To; Mart
Library

# 3 Generations of Success -Sicilian to American

Thank you

John B Belbeer

# 3 Generations of Success - Sicilian to American

✦

## Values for Immigrants and All Who Want to Succeed

*John Bellecci*

iUniverse, Inc.
New York   Bloomington

# 3 Generations of Success -Sicilian to American

## Values for Immigrants and All Who Want to Succeed

iUniverse books may be ordered through booksellers or by contacting:

iUniverse
1663 Liberty Drive
Bloomington, IN 47403
www.iuniverse.com
1-800-Authors (1-800-288-4677)

ISBN: 978-0-595-48464-5 (pbk)
ISBN: 978-0-595-60556-9 (ebk)

Printed in the United States of America

iUnverse rev. date: 11/18/08

# *Acknowledgments*

For Christmas of 1997, I was given pens, writing tablets, a tape recorder, and a promise to type whatever stories and narratives I delivered. I am most grateful to two of my daughters, Karen T. Baldwin and Lisa M. Bellecci-St.Romain, for the tremendous amount of work and planning that was done prior to submitting a draft to the printer in 1998. Also, this never would have been written without the encouragement to put these stories down on paper, coming from them and my three other daughters, Marian Bellecci, Linda Millburn, and Madeleine Timpa. In 1998, Madeleine and Lisa read and clarified the first tome. In 2006, Lisa had the idea for the new arrangement of these stories and did the work on this newly formatted version. Her daughter Theresa proofread the draft that went to the editor, Carole Honeychurch. Carole had good editorial suggestions, and Lisa carried out those, bringing this work to its present form.

My wife Ileane also needs to be thanked for her patience and support. She agreed to my postponing work around the house and yard while we wrote, rewrote, and rewrote again for months each time I approached this work.

I also want to thank the people who assisted in gathering the information for the genealogy charts, including my brother Frank Bellecci, my sister Marie Glazier, and my cousins, especially Tina Davi and Francine Grillo.

June, 2008

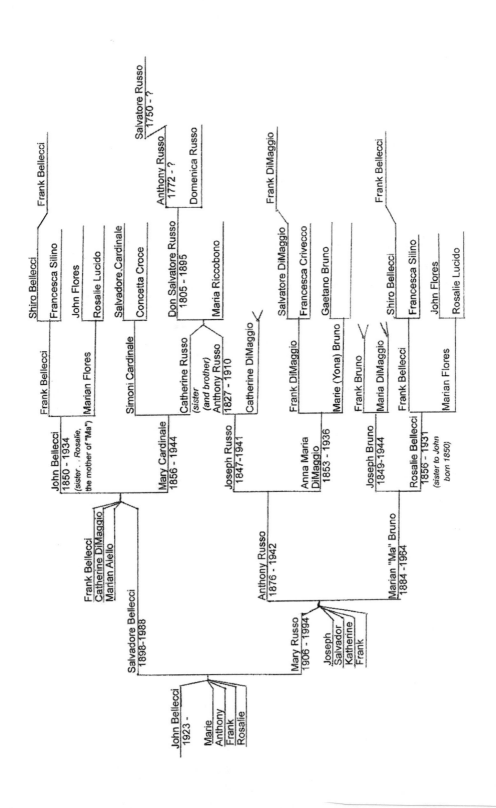

# Contents

# Introduction

My grandfather came from a long line of desperate men and women, but he wasn't related to them by blood. Rather, the experience of living as an immigrant connects him to many people, even those of thousands of years ago, migrating in various areas around the world. Today, in the United States, my grandfather has descendants in the new Hispanic and Asian immigrants.

What is it about immigrating that connects all these people? The desire for a better life for themselves and their families. The story of immigration, told and retold throughout centuries, is an exciting story, filled with adventurous people. It is a challenging story, filled with courageous actions and constant sacrifices. But above all, it is a story of hope and love. For most immigrants are members of families who seek to give their children and loved ones opportunities they never had, such as options in education, in work, and in developing their talents and skills to make the best life possible in the new country. Even forced immigrants to the United States, such as slaves and indentured servants or indentured farm laborers, desired a better life for their children.

## The Problem

However, immigrants are often unwanted by members of the country in which they seek to make a new life. Sometimes a love/hate relationship exists when the immigrant workforce is needed to do jobs that no one wants or is willing to do. I find it saddening and worrisome when I hear of negative feelings toward present-day immigrants to the United States, though I know that lack of documentation presents a dilemma. Still, many in our country seem to have forgotten that those in leadership now come from families who were once immigrants. This is a critical time in our country. Potential leaders need to be welcomed and mentored. We need help for our future together. I offer this book as part of that help.

# How to Use This Book

My family of immigrants has been successful in integrating with the citizens of the United States, while making better lives for ourselves and for our children. In writing this book, I share with you, the reader, how we achieved success by telling you stories of situations in which we were presented with critical choices. When we responded in these situations with honesty, integrity, strength, faith, courage, or perseverance, success followed.

I tell these stories to encourage you during your critical times. I hope you use the values to counsel and advise any family members, neighbors, church members, co-workers, or children in your care, anyone facing choices that might require a personal sacrifice for the sake of success. Refer often to these values to help focus energy toward true success. Though the century is different from that described in the stories, modern immigrants and other readers will understand how one can move toward success while adapting to the new culture and contributing to the success of the country, just as my family did.

The focus of this book, then, is to share what we have learned about the values that made many families successful, not just during the last one hundred or more years in America, but very likely throughout the history of humanity. These values promote and predict success and are the topics of the chapters in this book, illustrated with stories from the lives of the leaders in our family. I will use Chapter One to provide noteworthy background on the Bellecci family. The stories in Chapters Two through Eight are chosen to illustrate the specific values listed below:

Two: Stand up for yourself and your worth;

Three: Act with charity and integrity;

Four: Expect excellence, and put forth the effort;

Five: Hold no grudges;

Six: Take advantage of educational opportunities;

Seven: Have faith, and trust God.

And, since immigrants who hold these values and act on them consistently often become leaders, either formal or informal, in the community or in business, I include a chapter that contains stories of successful leadership decisions based on these values:

Eight: Manage with the Values.

# How This Book Can Help

If these values are fostered in each generation, they can immunize against invitations to join gangs. They help a person achieve a positive reputation and become a contributing member of society. Additionally, behaving according to these values can reduce the sense of threat perceived by members and leaders of the dominant culture, who appreciate the values of assertiveness, education, and striving for excellence. Those members and leaders can identify with integrity, with faith, and with the trials of grief that might cause one to stumble, but not fall.

My Bellecci grandfather was a man of great stature, both physically and intellectually, as well as in his community. He started us on the journey of integration; my father, and then I, learned by observation and followed suit. We were determined to succeed while being moral and honest, yet without allowing others to take undue advantage or continually mistreat us. Keeping the long-term view in mind, we were able to deflect hurts, delay gratification, and make tough decisions on the job, on family issues, and on the complexities of military life during my time in the service.

## About the Author

I was the first Italian from my town to attend college, graduating from one of the foremost universities of the time: the University of California at Berkeley. In my career as a chemical engineer, I moved up from a laboratory technician to supervisor and to plant manager, but only because I was willing to risk leaving a job without the future I envisioned. Working for several companies and sought by others, I finished my business career as the vice president of a Fortune 500 company. My two sisters, Marie Glazier and Rosalie Milano, and my brother Frank had similar initiative, holding jobs and starting their own businesses in real estate, civil engineering, and wholesale goods.

We jointly own commercial property in several states, something that we learned from our forebears in order to move ahead financially. Their strategy was to save as much as possible and invest it in rental properties, whether houses or commercial buildings; however, it will not work if you have more than you can manage, which detracts greatly from your quality of life. It also is necessary to invest only that money that is truly surplus (discretionary), so spouses and family members do not get anxious or want for necessary items. And it is best to maintain an attitude of patience, as not all investments pan out, and others take years to do so. We continue to count on this investment in land and buildings to further our financial success.

In our desire to keep learning more and giving of our talents, my wife Ileane and I, married almost sixty years, travel to various locations around the world, and we are active in our church. I consider this a very successful life. It is all the more satisfying when I consider how my children, nieces, and nephews have flourished.

Frank, Rosalie, and I have thirteen children among us, to whom we and Marie have worked to transmit the values in this book. They turned out to be responsible citizens and contributing members of society. All attended college, with several earning advanced degrees. They took advantage of educational opportunities and now work in the following fields: medicine (two doctors and one nurse), civil engineering, teaching (one elementary teacher and one university adjunct professor), surveying, drafting, accounting, computer programming, social work, pastoral ministry (a second career), financial advising, and commercial property management. Among other accomplishments, they have established or expanded businesses, published books, patented inventions, and designed a golf course.

Yet success is more than one's place in the business world. It is also about relationships. Our next generation has not lost sight of this important aspect of life. Though cousins, they support each other like brothers and sisters. They enjoy each other's company, visit regularly and at family reunions, remember important dates through a family e-mail list, and keep in close contact though they live in scattered parts of the country. Family has remained important for them.

The subsequent generation includes our grandchildren, nineteen altogether, in the process of finding their way from grade school to employment. We have already seen their successes as they finish college and contribute to society, again guided by these same values. So far we have an elementary teacher and public historian/editor, graduating cum laude and magna cum laude, respectively; a graphic artist; and a bilingual med student who became a member of Phi Beta Kappa as a college junior and graduated summa cum laude. The other grandchildren are en route to success with aims as varied as surveying, mechanical engineering, theology, the priesthood, accounting, architecture, computer science, hotel management, and makeup artistry. And still another generation has begun, as two great-grandchildren have been born to our family.

We credit the values detailed in this book as the foundation for each generation's continued success. We have retained our Italian heritage and aspects of the Italian culture that are important to us, yet we have integrated as Americans. What has worked for us can work for immigrants of all kinds-- those newly arrived and those whose families have been here for generations.

Someone just has to tell the stories. In my case, hearing the stories began early in my life.

# The First Story

When I was very young, my grandfather John would take me on walks on the streets in Martinez, California. We usually went into the Costanza General Store. There I would be given the opportunity to select some goodie to eat on the way back to his house. On one of these trips, when I was at most six years old, we met a friend of my grandfather's who was very happy to meet grandfather's descendant of the same name, John.

He exclaimed: "This young boy is going to be special. He needs to know his heritage and how he must act in the future."

Then, though my grandfather made some protests, his friend proceeded to tell me the very important occurrence of when a Mafioso came from San Francisco to Martinez to shake down the local fishermen. The Mafia man knew that most of the Italian immigrants in Martinez had arrived between 1898 and 1904; it was not necessary to obtain entry papers. Hence the term WOP for those Italians who were "Without Papers" but were perfectly legal entrants to the USA. (It was not until after 1906 that entry visas were needed.) However, he, the stranger, told these Martinez fishermen that since they didn't have papers, they were illegally in the USA. If they didn't pay him, he would turn them in to be jailed or deported.

Grandfather's friend continued with the story: "As the Mafioso pressed for his quiet money, the fishermen, trusting their friend to lead them in this, finally said, 'You get John Bellecci to pay, and we will pay too. John Bellecci is in Pittsburg, fifteen miles distant today, but he will be back next Sunday, our normal repair day.' The next Sunday, sure enough, the extortionist was back looking for your grandfather, John Bellecci. The Mafioso found your grandfather and explained that the facts of life in the new country were just like in Sicily." The storyteller said that my grandfather knew everyone in the local town was aware that he despised the Mafia. My grandfather, therefore, thought this was a joke that the other fishermen were playing on him. But then, it wasn't long before my grandfather John realized this was no joke. The discussion became heated.

Grandfather's friend came to the point of pride, saying, "We were all at the racks, thirty to fifty yards away, but we heard your grandfather, without his lips moving, tell the man, as he picked him up off his feet, 'If I ever see you again, I'll kill you.' And then your grandfather threw him. The man got up and began running, never to return."

This event ensured that life in America would really be better than Sicily. The fishermen already saw my grandfather as a leader. They counted on his size, his personality, his intense determination, and his loyalty to the whole community. The threat of violence seemed necessary to get the message across to the ruthless group back in San Francisco.

I was told many more stories when they saw how eagerly and closely I listened. From that story and the others, I learned of my grandfather's courage, his integrity, and his willingness to do what was right for his own good and for order in the community. I saw firsthand the trust the others had in him. Later, I noted that they also admired my father, Salvador, whom they distinguished from other men named Salvador in the community by the use of the respectful nickname "Salvaturino." Let's turn now to some background information on the Belleccis, to help you know how the family story began, and to understand the culture and behavior in the stories of this book.

# Chapter One: Background

This chapter provides background on immigration, on my family, and on the Italian culture so as to better appreciate and understand the more detailed stories to come. Many of us remember hearing the adage: "Those who do not learn from history are doomed to repeat it." Often we rolled our eyes, because history was usually taught as a series of wars and battles, and it did not seem that anyone had learned anything. But a fuller grasp of the story of human life on earth shows us predictable and repeating patterns in cultures. Conflict or trouble in various forms caused people to consider the risky move away from their homeland into a new area that was populated by strangers who often spoke a different language.

Why would someone leave familiar places and the people they knew (and usually loved) to settle in the fearful unknown? The desire to make such a move falls into one of two categories: either people feel "pushed" out by problems in their native land, or they feel "pulled" toward a new land, drawn by attractive opportunities. In reading the news or listening to reports today, we find these two powerful forces are still common. Situations that can push people out of their country are war, hunger, crowding, politics, religious intolerance, lack of work, or abuse from those around them. People who are in such troubling situations will find political stability, tolerance, and the perception of being able to improve one's income, employment, and education as great attractions for moving. Still, it takes great courage to actually make the move, to leave the familiar, even if it holds so much pain. My grandfather's reasons for leaving were lack of work in Sicily and an unstable political situation, while the draw to America was its reputation of having many employment opportunities.

## *Troubling Contact*

Moving to the new area did not magically solve the immigrant's problems. Once in contact, the people of the two interacting cultures faced dilemmas concerning intermarriage (especially common when the men moving in outnumbered the women), as well as due to the different practices in religion, government, family structure, and decision making. The gender structure might be different, including variation in laws allowing women to own property, to receive an education, and the like. Societies might differ in the formation of castes or social classes. Unfortunately, when physical immunities differed, diseases were also shared, some of which were deadly to each other. But if the peoples of the two cultures managed to work through these issues positively, it meant continued progress toward a new and mutually enriched culture.

## *The Bellecci Contact*

My grandfather was already married, so he was not looking for a wife in the new land. The same Catholic religion was available to him and his generation, but parts of the Mass, the worship service, were not in his language. The laws in the new country should have protected him, but since the police and courts did not know his language, he and the other Italian immigrants were often without immediate help; hence, his position of leadership and his choice to use the tactic of threatening physical violence. Regarding gender structure, women in Sicily could own property, as they could at that time in the United States. The women in my family took advantage of this in both countries and were financially quite successful. (In Sicily, the women traditionally kept their maiden name as well.) Regarding infectious diseases, I am not aware of any problems that my grandfather's generation encountered in the United States; the flu epidemic of his son's (my father's) generation was worldwide.

What proved to be the very best difference between the two cultures was the widespread access to public education in the new country. I learned in no uncertain terms that education and respectful behavior in school were very important, from my childhood on to college. A college education would never have been available to those in my family in Sicily; in the United States, I received a very good college education and then gave back to this society for over forty years, making a difference in the business world with solid performance.

# The Bellecci Background

A different culture can offer others many insights, deep enrichment, and an expanded horizon. When one culture is able to welcome and incorporate the gifts of another culture, both are enhanced. Our clan has a very varied genetic background with some women and men of average height while others are as much as six inches taller. Some have been blond and blue eyed, or redheads with brown eyes; others had black hair and fair skin or olive coloration.

In Sicily, it was unusual to find this much variation in just one family. After genealogical searching, we learned why. My sister and cousins found an ancestor who was not Sicilian at all. Four generations back on my father's side, and five generations back on my mother's side was Don Salvatore Russo, an adopted immigrant son. Welcoming him into the family brought great enrichment to his parents and those who followed. This is how it occurred.

Sometime between 1810 and 1820, a young boy was left at the doorstep of Anthony Russo and his wife Domenica (her last name is unknown to us), who lived in a coastal town of Sicily called Isola della Femina. It seems that a Norwegian ship made port at Isola and, after several days, left in the night, unknown to the villagers. The Russos could not find out where the ship was headed next, and no one ever returned or sent an inquiry about this little redheaded boy who spoke the strange Germanic tongue that no Sicilian really understood. The Russos had no children of their own, and when they tried to give the boy to the orphanage, the authorities refused to accept him. They had too many orphans already, due to a constant stream of children left fatherless since France (which controlled Sicily) was conscripting young men to fight in Africa for the French Foreign Legion.

The Russos kept the boy at the request of the authorities. What a fortunate decision. This single involuntary immigrant came to be loved not only by his new parents, who named him Salvatore, but also by the people of the village. His parents trained him according to their values of honesty and responsibility.

Salvatore grew up to be the mayor of the village with an administration so extraordinarily honest that he was reelected for many terms. He was extremely frugal; in fact, he was probably a tightwad, but he was phenomenally energetic. He was very tall and slim and seemed to continually patrol the village. His restaurant was immaculate, though he spent little time there. He became wealthy, and the village prospered during his tenure. He and his wife, Maria, had two children, a boy, Anthony, and a girl, Catherina. Catherina Russo married Simoni Cardinale, and they became my father's grandparents. Anthony Russo married Catherine DiMaggio—my mother's great-grandparents. Thus, in an unusual turn of events, this one involuntary immigrant, Don Salvatore, influenced many people of both of my parents' families, as he was their common ancestor.

My grandfather John Bellecci was born in 1849 in that town of Isola della Femina, near Palermo in Sicily. He grew up in a time of political turmoil. The city-states on the peninsula of Italy were going through a unification process under the control of Garibaldi, and Sicily was being removed from the control of Spain and France. Anarchy reigned from 1860 to 1875, and the Mafia had opportunity to begin organizing. But even in the midst of turmoil, people fell in love and desired to marry.

The custom at that time was for parents to arrange the marriages, usually with input from the son or daughter, as they considered a suitor from among the set of local young people. John's parents, being relatively well-to-do fisherfolk, had the pick of the young women in the small town. It did not hurt that John was very tall (six feet) and fairly good-looking and had a reputation for being industrious and intelligent. He was certain to have his own boat and crew in a short time, important signs of wealth.

But before letting him accumulate his own goods, his parents wanted him married. Until then, his mother would collect his earnings, as was customary for a single man living at home. Then she would dole out that money to all of the children, adults or minors, as she thought necessary. Though young men negotiated additional bar and entertainment money, self-management was understandably an incentive to young men to marry.

John's parents had selected one of the village belles as his wife without consulting him, and her parents were agreeable to the match. Surprisingly, John was not. After considerable discussion and delays, his parents understood that he was in love with the daughter of a local bar and restaurant owner. John's parents had a problem with her very poor eyesight, as they assumed she would not be a good housekeeper. (At that time in Sicily, eyeglasses were not commonly available; in the few instances when they were, they were effectively only a magnifying glass.) John did not care about eyesight or housekeeping. He withstood the withering fire of his persistent mother, the customs of the town, the expectations of the townspeople and the chosen young woman, and the frustration of his own siblings. He was intent on marrying the woman he truly wanted, Marietta "Marutza" Cardinale. Because he was holding up the other matches of his two younger sisters and brothers (by custom, the oldest married first), his mother finally capitulated. This is the first of many instances that we know of in which he insisted upon having his way in a serious life decision. Such a trait of assertiveness would repeat several times in the United States. But how did he happen to settle there?

# The Temporary Job in the New Country

John and Marutza had two daughters, Marian and Catherine, and adopted a son, Frank, within their first four years of marriage. Unfortunately, the fishing gradually went sour. With this growing family to provide for, my grandfather decided to leave the Mediterranean and live in the United States for a few years, with the vision of making a lot of money. They planned that he would send the majority of his earnings back to his wife, Marutza, who would begin to acquire property in Isola, Sicily.

Though surely an adventure for him, this was also a sacrifice for the family as he was leaving the wife he had fought for, and Marutza would be alone raising the children. Once fishing improved, he would come back to the Mediterranean. With the purchases of land Marutza could make with his money, they would be wealthy when he arrived home.

In this temporary work-away plan, John followed typical immigration practices of hundreds of years, that of sending a moneymaker to the new land, while keeping the family anchored in the familiar territory, not really intending to make a permanent move. Also typical was that, on his first visit to America, he moved to a location where other Sicilians were already established. In this instance, he joined the fruit and vegetable peddlers in the city of St. Louis. This piggybacking on the accomplishments of settled immigrants is a wise step in immigration, since the newcomer does not know the language or customs of the new country.

Fortunately, John was not too proud to join the established peddling trade, even though it was not his first preference of employment. He lived frugally, continually sending earnings back home. Though this practice of sending money to the family back home is often condemned in the present day because it disrupts the cycle of local spending, it has been going on for generations. Many times it is a prelude to the more permanent step of moving the whole family, which brings added benefits to the economic cycle.

# The Move to the New Country

In John's case, the "few years" he was gone became fifteen. When he finally arrived back in Sicily about 1897, he shifted to fishing for sponges on the islands around Sicily, since world demand generated good prices. He had reunited with his wife, and they had a son in 1898, Salvador, my father.

Unfortunately, during the years John was in America, the Mafia had maintained and even expanded its power, ruling over the working classes and extorting money from the shopkeepers. Within just a few years, John had enough of their domination. In 1902, he decided tolerating or giving in to the Mafia was not a practice he wanted to continue. This is another example of his refusal to be pushed around. His sense of justice required him to stand up for himself and his family. They sold the property Marutza had bought, and they moved away from the Mafia repression in Sicily, taking the whole family to the United States.

They made their new home in California, again a place in which many Sicilians had already located. While many acquaintances lived in Black Diamond (now Pittsburg), John's wife Marutza insisted on living in a town that wasn't a "muddy swamp" all winter, as Black Diamond often became. She wanted the more appealing environment of sidewalks and was willing to sacrifice having sure acquaintances nearby. They chose the town of Martinez instead, northeast of San Francisco, with waterway access for fishing. It was graced with wooden sidewalks on Main Street and had a house the family could own, on Escobar Street, just one block off Main Street. They used money from the sale of their property in Sicily to pay for it. They were happy; they were eager to make their life in the new country.

Grandfather John, vigorous, healthy, muscular, and tall, eventually came to be the unofficial leader of the fishing community. Though he never learned English, he earned a position as leader for the immigrants mainly due to consistent success in his work and his willingness to act swiftly and decisively on ethical and moral issues. He, and many in the family after him, would not allow bullying in the community, nor would they do what went against a sense of justice, even if family members were not the ones who would suffer ultimately. We've already seen John's reaction to the Mafia's attempt to establish in Martinez. The next chapter holds more stories that illustrate the value of standing up for oneself.

# Chapter Two: Stand Up for Yourself and Your Worth

As we've seen so far, John's story of succeeding in his native Italy and then taking a temporary job in America involved his strength of will, his sense of duty, and his perseverance in the face of opposition. These are all important traits for an immigrant or anyone seeking success in America. Another important factor in achieving success in this country is the ability and the willingness to stand up for oneself.

All of us experience opposition to what we want, and this might be especially true of new immigrants. The language barrier might be overwhelming, or the total cooperation that the people of the new country expect of you might not be in your best interest. Grandfather John used his belief in himself and his unwillingness to be pushed aside to spur him on in his new country, as he had in his native land.

## Helping the Hobos

When helping another person, we usually have in mind the kind and extent of help we are able to give. But what do you do when the other wants more? Maybe you decide to give a little more, but perhaps what the other requests is reaching too far. You must assess the situation quickly, considering whether it seems to be a one-time request or is likely to set up a pattern of the other repeatedly taking advantage of you. Take into account the resources and abilities of the other to fill his or her own needs in the future. My grandfather and my mother had two different experiences of helping the hobos who encamped for many years in the Martinez area. Here are their stories.

Grandfather John worked as a fisherman in his new home in Martinez, selling some of his catch and bartering with the local farmers, both Italian and Japanese. Periodically he would carry a gunnysack full of fish to Port Costa, about three miles east, to sell there. The path he walked followed the railroad track, laid down along the shores of the Carquinez Straits. (The Carquinez Straits is a narrow channel carrying water from two inland rivers emptying into the San Francisco Bay. Hills rise steeply from the shoreline.) On one visit to Port Costa, he returned with a few fish in his sack still unsold. As he walked back home, he neared the slough where the fishing boats were moored and where a campground lay, called the Hobo Camp. Passing by the camp, he thought: *These hobos could use some fresh fish*, so he offered his fish to the four or five men he saw there. They said "Sure!" to his offer of the fish, then added, "We'll have your money, too."

John told them in English, "Fish, yes; money, no," but they decided they would just take the money from him. However, John was a very strong six-footer: though there were four hobos, they turned out to be no match for him. Two of them were injured to the point of needing hospital attention. At the hospital, the hobos told the medical personnel that it was a whole group of fishermen who had suddenly attacked them.

The next day, the police came to investigate at the racks where the nets were laid out, asking the reason why several fishermen would pick on these hobos. The whole community had already heard the story by the next morning, and they told the police it was only one person, John Bellecci, who was defending himself. John, for his part, said through an interpreter that he had been willing to share his extra food but not the money for which he had worked hard. That was for his family. One did not surrender what was for his family. He felt he had been justified in defending himself, rather than turning the money over. The police left, laughing as they told the fishermen that they wouldn't be bothered anymore.

The hobos assumed that "might made right"—that having a group of four meant they could steal and take what they wanted. Grandfather John did not know if he could defeat them, but he was willing to take the blows necessary to keep the money that would provide for his family. His split-second decision was informed by courage and the principle of standing up for himself.

The hobo camp was a regular landmark, thanks to the local railroad switch-off point. In later times, during the depression of the 1930s and early 40s, and most frequently in the wintertime, hobos in need approached individual family homes. When they came to our house, my mother had quite a different experience of them, which was probably more typical for people than my grandfather's. They politely asked her if she had some work around the yard or house they could do in exchange for food and clothes. She found a little job for every one of the hobos who came and accepted their work without any fear or concern for the family's well-being.

My father was concerned about her safety. She assured him of the firm boundaries she set: she never let them come in the house and never gave money. My mother would tell him, "They are poor people, they need help, and it doesn't cost us anything." That was my grandfather's thinking as well. But both still set boundaries on the circumstances of how they would help. None of the hobos ever made any threat to my mother, and they were always appreciative.

## *Protecting the Livelihood*

In those days, it was necessary to police one's own area because the town had only two police officers, certainly not enough for the whole populace, and in any case, neither spoke Italian. When he needed to, Grandfather John took the job of enforcer of the ethical code of conduct in the Italian community. The other men in the community looked to him and supported him in that role as best as they could.

This lack of strong policing in an immigrant community, whether due to language or cultural barriers, is unfortunately a common aspect of the process of becoming part of the dominant culture. Leaders from within immigrant groups, both formal and informal, are called upon to prevent chaos in their communities. In the following story, you will notice that John did give warning to the offenders, though they chose not to abide by the established rules. When John did resort to aggressive responses, he focused only on those who broke the basic rule of respect for others, thus enabling orderly life to continue. We know of no situation in which he engaged in personal vengeance, nor did he ever use his strength or threat of violence for personal gain based on the work of others, as the Mafia enforcers wanted to do. In this story, he simply wanted to protect the orderly system of making a livelihood.

How do many fishermen all manage to fish at once, when the shad or the salmon are running and everyone is in a rush to acquire all the fish that they can? In fishing at the Carquinez Straits, there was a protocol for lining up, "first come, first in line," which held for each drift of the tides. This was the standard practice, and the way to get ahead was to sacrifice sleep or to make a more powerful motor so your boat could get in line faster—or sometimes to do both.

However, a particular family from Pittsburg had a rebellious son who decided to ignore the rule. While the other men got up early to get to their place in line, waiting for the tides, this "cheater" would show up late and put his boat in front of the first one. Though they had sometimes been in place for hours, the men tended to excuse the cheater's behavior by saying, "Oh, he's young." or "He's just dumb." Perhaps they recalled their own youth, when they tested the limits. Perhaps they thought he would wise up and follow the rules once his family heard what he was doing. Perhaps they did not want to make waves. Whatever the reason, several times the rebel got away with this behavior (called "caulking"), usurping the position of those who respected the orderly process.

My Grandfather John spent money every year to get the most speed possible out of his boat, in order to be able to get to that first position before the others when moving from one area of drift to the next. (In a twenty-four-hour period, the fishermen had six or eight opportunities to catch the drift first.) The first position was important because that fishing net caught the first rush of the tide, thus getting the best opportunity for salmon, while the others behind the first fisherman got only the fish that managed to get by or around.

On the occasion when the cheater cut his boat in front of my grandfather and started laying out his net, effectively stealing the best drift, my grandfather told my Uncle Frank, his elder son, to steer the boat toward the interlopers. Arriving near them, John told them clearly and concisely, that their cutting in line was not the way to act in Martinez; they were not to do it again.

The Bellecci boat sailed off, but by now it had a very poor position for netting salmon on that night. The next night, the cheater was back again. John yelled at them to pull up or suffer the consequences. They laughed at him. Big mistake. "Frank, speed up the boat; I'll take the rudder," my grandfather ordered my uncle. He headed straight at the violating boat, ramming it broadside. It sank. Still infuriated, John picked up his oar and began beating the cheater and his crew while they floundered in the water. Eventually, they were pulled out of the water by others.

In the morning, as the Belleccis brought their fish to market, the police arrested John and put him in jail. He refused to pay bail; he refused to pay any fine; and he absolutely refused to pay for damages. Through an interpreter in court, he asked the judge if he, the judge, would be willing to pay for injuring robbers who came into the judge's house to rob him. When the court adjourned, John was sent back to jail. The next day he was released and was told somebody paid his fine. He was never able to determine who had done so.

My grandfather was willing to take the consequences of his aggressive behavior; it was worth it to communicate to the young man and to the family that had not taught or would not teach him to respect the rules. Still, with each new generation, the rules had to be made clear. A generation later, my father encountered the same situation in the fishing lineup. A certain renegade in the fishing community would jump in line ahead of those in front of him. When he did this to my father, Dad drove his boat toward the interloper and threatened him physically for that action. He not only told him that should he never again do that, but he also directed the crew to pick up the nets immediately and get in line correctly. The interloper disrespectfully dismissed my father, but *his* father, who was the partner in his boat, started to pick up. He knew of my grandfather's actions under similar circumstances.

What is it that makes one person willing to stand up for himself or herself when others do not? Perhaps it is a heightened sense of justice and injustice. Maybe it is what one is passionate about, as making a living is to the man who has a family to support. In the next story, we'll see how my father's new wife, herself a young girl, used the fury of her passion for her baby to assert herself.

## Get Support to Make Your Point

Those people who do not have much power must find someone who has more power, or is looked upon with more respect, in order to achieve their goal. My mother was only sixteen when she married my father, who was eight years older. (I was born the year after their wedding.) Due to her age and the culture of the time, she must have felt little power.

My father was in the habit of visiting his parents every evening. This was a common custom of the time, indicating the high value the Italians placed on being in close contact with one's family. He took me with him regularly, even as an infant. When I was six months old, my Grandfather John happened to give me a taste of a brandy-soaked peach, and since I understandably wanted more, he kept letting me suck on them during the visit. Busily engaged in conversation with my father, enjoying my delight in sucking on the peaches, and not thinking about the effects of even that little amount of alcohol on a baby, he effectively gave me enough to get me drunk. When my father brought me home that evening, my mother was aghast at my lolling head and the smell of brandy on me. She immediately took me and left the house, going to her parents' home a short distance away, where she stayed for the night. Her terms for return: that my father would never take me to his parents' house again! My father was stunned. He could not imagine fulfilling that wish, but his wife's mind was made up, young girl or not. She was immovable, and she had left his home.

Fortunately, his mother-in-law, a cousin and known to the family as a businesswoman and friend, was very practical and level-headed. She knew I would need to be able to go to my paternal grandparents' home. She convinced my mother that she was in a position of power, and it was to her advantage to negotiate. Both she and my mother were back at home the next day, to tell my father that he could take me to his parents' home, but they were *never* to give me brandied peaches or cherries, or any kind of alcohol again. My father and his parents quickly agreed to the women's requirements, grateful for a second chance.

My mother gained power in this situation, due to her willingness to address an issue about which she felt strongly, but also because of her willingness to negotiate rather than stubbornly following through on a threat made in the heat of anger. Having my grandmother with her enhanced her bargaining position. No one dared to chastise her for leaving her husband's house or for making the drastic threat.

## *The Fine Line*

Sometimes one notices children who have a sense of assertiveness and self-sufficiency that surprises the adults. It is important not to grind such children down, while still stressing their obligation to treat others with respect.

My parents settled into a home close to my maternal grandmother, as my young mother relied on her help in many ways. When I was a child, I used to pass by Curry's Mortuary, which was on the street between my mother's and grandmother's house. Since I willingly engaged anyone in conversation (my nickname from early childhood was John Continente, which means "John who says nothing" because I never stopped talking), the men who worked at Curry's would converse with me about shopping and my grandmother's bread baking, usually giving me sweets. They were Irish and liked to tease me about my freckles, telling me I must not be Italian, I must be adopted.

Once I went home and asked what adopted meant. Stunned, and then angry, I went right back and really let them have it! Imagine a five year-old reading the riot act to three adult men! They laughed so hard they could not stop. I just stomped off.

After that, though, they did not tease me so much and actually let me go into the room where the coffins and cadavers were. I told my mother about the people sleeping in the rooms. She told me I should not go in there, because those people would never wake up. Mr. Curry told me that as long as I was quiet, it was all right to look at them. I am grateful that those men were willing to treat even a young child with some amount of respect and act as a kind of mentor to me.

## Refusing to Support Incompetence

What do you do when it seems that your boss is not competent, and you believe you are being asked to do something that is unwise or possibly harmful? The situation might be compounded by your experience and your boss's lack of it. Speaking up at work might be appreciated, or it might give you the reputation of being uncooperative. When you do speak up, be sure to back up your claim with as many facts as possible about how the company is in jeopardy. Your own personal feelings of hurt or rejection will not sway the administrators, but if you phrase the problem so as to point out that the company or business stands to lose customers or reputation, then you are in a better position.

My father, who worked for over fifteen years at one company, found himself unsupported by administration when his supervisor repeatedly displayed incompetence. In the early 1940s, during World War II, my dad worked as the foreman of maintenance and repair at Pioneer Rubber Mills in Pittsburg, California. During the war, a nationwide law forbade people in essential industries from changing jobs, to keep companies from raiding skilled workers from other companies. Pioneer Mills had hired an electrical engineer to oversee the installation of automatic equipment as the company transitioned to making fire hoses for the navy. When this task was done, they needed to give him more work and made him the supervisor over the maintenance department, including Dad, the foreman. Dad let the management know that this supervisor did not know as much about maintenance and repair as he himself did. They encouraged Dad to be patient. The fellow stayed mostly out of the way, so initially Dad thought it would not be too bad.

One day, however, when Dad had assigned two men to a job that required one man to look and signal, while the other fellow worked an electric hoist, the new boss came upon the scene. The supervisor saw one fellow just yelling to his counterpart, not looking busy. Not understanding what was going on, but worse, not asking, he told the up-man to go to another job. The remaining man subsequently was injured.

Dad was called on the carpet by higher management for using unsafe procedures when he should have known better. They thought he had assigned only one worker to the job, but Dad did not know that one of his men had been removed. He responded that two men had done that job fifty times with no problem. He just could not understand what was so unsafe or what the up-man had done wrong to allow the other one to get injured.

During this correctional meeting that went on for two hours, Dad's supervisor was present but never said a word about removing the second man. The vice president, who had known Dad for ten years or more, eventually came in and chided Dad about the "not too smart shortcuts that we're taking." Dad defended himself, stating there was no shortcut. He suggested the vice president call on the injured worker. The higher-ups did so and, during questioning, learned that Dad's new boss had taken the up-man off the job. Not only had the new boss made the error, he also had just sat in the room without admitting his responsibility while Dad got grilled during that two-hour meeting.

Immediately, as that information came to light, Dad told the vice president, the superintendent, the plant manager, and everybody else in that room, "I no longer report to Idiot, or I quit." This ultimatum my father delivered in the heat of anger, but he was not one to tolerate incompetence. Still, giving an ultimatum to your boss is very risky and should only be done if you have a backup plan.

They reminded him, "You can't quit. Pioneer is an essential war industry." This proved to be a mistaken tactic, telling Dad what he could or could not do. They continued: "If you don't work for us, you can't work for anybody." They warned him that he could not make a living.

However, he countered that assumption. "I can too. I can fish, and I can take party boats out." Dad refused to cooperate when the system was not interested in correcting incompetence. He then asked to use their phone.

"Sure, go ahead." He called home. It happened that, as the phone rang, I had just walked in the door from taking a final exam at the University of California at Berkeley. Mom was startled to receive the call, but did not question her husband.

"What? Yes, he just came in. All right." She hung up the phone and told me, "You and I are driving to Pittsburg to get your father." I knew something must be wrong; I thought that he must be hurt. In the fifteen years Dad worked at Pioneer, we had never picked him up in the middle of the day. I asked my mother if he was hurt. She did not know, but she could tell he was very angry. It was a very quiet ride. I got there as quickly as I could.

When I drove up to the rubber mill, we could see Dad standing on the side of the street, arms crossed, overalls rolled into a bundle on the ground next to his lunch box and toolbox. We pulled up. Usually when going for a ride in the car, he would have Mom get out of the front seat and move to the back so *he* could sit in the front. (This was the tradition; the older person or one with more status got to sit up front with the driver.) But Dad did not wait for her to move this time; he got in the backseat, loaded in his equipment, and simply directed me, "Go home."

The vice president and superintendent stood on the side of the street, imploring Mom to get him to change his mind. They told her that they could not let him work anywhere else. She knew her husband's temperament and wisely replied, "He doesn't interfere in the house; I don't interfere in his work. It's up to him to do what he wants to do." They followed tradition and had two separate spheres; she knew he was extremely responsible and would cover his part of providing for the family.

A few days later, Dad went to have lunch with some friends in the Yuba Manufacturing Shop in Benicia, which is across the Carquinez straits from Martinez. When his friends found out he was not working, they first gave him the spiel about loyalty to the US war effort. Soon, however, they realized the situation and then felt delighted. Dad was a first-class machinist before he was twenty, and now, twenty-five years later, his friends knew there was not another unemployed machinist anywhere near Benicia who could "carry his toolbox." They brought the plant manager into the lunchroom to try to persuade Dad to work in their shop. As a former gold-dredger manufacturing plant, the Yuba plant was desperately short of labor as it now struggled to produce 155 mm howitzer barrels for the navy. They were drastically behind schedule and needed help. Dad reminded them that the rubber mill had a top priority on people, and they were not going to release him to work anywhere else.

When the Yuba hierarchy understood the situation, they called Mare Island Naval Base for authority to hire Dad. Amazingly, they received a release for Dad. Before going to work at Yuba, Dad extracted a contract from them which allowed him to receive special time off of four to six weeks in the spring and fall for commercial fishing, as well as an incentive add-on to his hourly rate if he reduced or eliminated the backlog. Yuba knew his reputation and agreed to everything. Thanks to Dad again standing up for his worth, this was a profitable arrangement for both sides. However, this expression of confidence by Yuba was only possible because Dad had been willing to leave his secure job over the issue of an incompetent supervisor.

An ironic situation occurred ten or eleven years later. I encountered that same supervisor who had sat by and let Dad take the blame for removing one of the workers. He was working as an equipment storeroom clerk at Stauffer Chemical Company, where I was superintendent of fertilizers. That man recognized the name of Bellecci on an order and came to talk to me. He wanted to express his concern about my father having quit the rubber mill.

I told him that, contrary to his concern, my father's decision then had led to one of the best breaks of his whole life.

After the man left, I surmised that his present job level of clerk indicated that he must not have done well in learning the kinds of responsibility and initiative that were expected of a supervisor. When I told Dad I had met him and what his present position was, Dad simply replied, "That's about what he's good for."

## *Standing Up to Those You Love*

To assert oneself with one's own parents may be the biggest challenge of one's life. In the Italian culture, as in others, respect for elders is foundational. To stand up to an adult is often interpreted as disrespect. Additionally, the dependence on parents one feels in childhood is hard to overcome. Many adults are still in the habit of striving for parental approval and love. As the oldest child, I often bore the brunt of extremely high expectations, being chastised or ridiculed for incorrectly doing something in which I had never been instructed. My father had not earned his reputation by being sloppy. He was a perfectionist, and it showed up in all aspects of his life. From early childhood and on, I had these corrections so often that, with my father, I would not argue. My sister Marie also felt the same high expectations and similar constraints as the oldest girl. The pressures were not so strong on our younger siblings.

Once, when I was a young man and my brother Frank an older teen, he and I were helping renovate the walls on a house we had moved from Martinez to Concord for my newly married sister Marie. (It was a house Mom and Dad owned in the town of Martinez. We moved it to property that Marie's husband had in Concord.) But as the day wore on, Dad's very critical eye was too much for Frank. After several corrections, which Frank thought were far too picky, and some verbal ridicule by Dad, my brother threw down his tools, shouted, "Well, if you don't like it, then just do it yourself!" and left the site. Frank was on foot, but that did not matter to him. He walked the entire eight miles back home to Martinez. His insubordination was never discussed that I know of, and Frank was treated with more respect after that. I watched with incredulity and always admired my younger brother for being able to stand up for himself with our father.

# Don't Be Afraid to Use the System

The military, like any bureaucracy, is often unable to be responsive to an individual's special need, since it is designed to function efficiently handling large numbers of people. In that type of organization, it is best to assert oneself not by asking for special attention, but by drawing attention to the rules that might have been violated. Use the hierarchical arrangement, and go over someone's head. This kind of assertiveness is necessary when dealing with bureaucrats who are not in a position to grant favors but who will do what their higher-ups order. I learned about this from my parents, who interacted with many bureaucracies in their life.

I joined the military after one and a half years in college at UC Berkeley. I knew the government was drafting young men at the age of twenty-one, and I decided to join early with the hope of negotiating the terms. We made the agreement that I would not be called up for at least six months (so I could finish my sophomore year), and I would also receive more education in the army. I did finish my sophomore year before they called me in. I went through basic training and then, because of my army test scores and college courses in engineering and the sciences, was sent to Clemson for courses in construction engineering. That excellent program closed after the second term, so I was assigned to an engineering pipeline company at Camp Claiborne in Louisiana. By now I had been in the army for a year, but when it became known that I could speak Italian, I was sent to Tulsa and worked an additional stint as an Italian translator, coordinating between American scientists and our allies.

The rule in the military was that after one year in service, all GIs within the United States could take a furlough to their home, if they wished. The typical length of a furlough was ten days at home, with up to six days of traveling time. In my case, my furlough was overdue after training and three months on extended duty at Tulsa University. All the other members of the 1383rd Engineering Pipeline Company to which I had been assigned had already completed their furloughs. When I arrived back in Louisiana from Tulsa and asked for mine, I was told I could only have a total of ten days (travel time included). Since travel was done via train, to go and come back would have taken nine days, maybe longer. I refused to leave under those circumstances. I insisted on receiving the ten days at home due to me. After advising the executive officer that I would go see the chaplain for this mistreatment, he came up with an alternative: flying me back and forth to San Francisco, a means of travel usually reserved for the upper echelon officers. I gladly accepted this arrangement. Traveling by plane was much preferable to days on a train.

I flew from Alexandria, Louisiana, to El Paso, Texas, to Phoenix, Arizona, to Los Angeles, California, and finally landed in San Francisco, twenty-four hours after starting. I was nearly always the only enlisted man on the plane, for which I received some snide remarks and stares. I felt no obligation to explain. Upon arrival in San Francisco, I asked the noncom officer in charge of flight scheduling if he would postpone my return trip for one day. He said it was no problem. He had authority to do so up to three days. Again, working within the system paid off for me.

When I got back to Camp Claiborne in Louisiana, the executive officer saw me and told me to get the "x#@*%" out to California (my furlough destination), or else I would be in the brig for the duration of the war. I informed him I had just returned from ten days at home. They had not even missed me. I never did figure out why he was so hesitant to let me have all the travel and furlough days to which I was entitled, but I was very glad I had asserted myself and gotten what was overdue.

## *Risking Court-Martial*

When you have some particular training or information, good citizenship and Christian values suggest that you use this training for the common good. But what if the people in command do not listen? The following story is about another army incident in which I needed to act assertively, not for myself but for the war effort. I was a young private, just twenty-two years old, without any status, but I was desperate to have someone in authority listen to me. I decided to use a shock tactic—inviting court-martial. It did get attention.

While I was serving in the army in New Guinea, I had just come off night duty when Sergeant Benes came to the tent and woke me up, only thirty minutes after I had gone to sleep. "Now what?" I grumbled.

"We're going to lay a water line. Everybody out," he says.

"Water line? Where?" I managed to mumble.

"From the dock to the storage tank farm," he answered.

"I'm not going," I told him, more alert now. The storage tanks were for gasoline. Why they wanted to get water from the dock *to* the gas storage tanks was beyond me, but I knew we did not want to mix gas and water.

"This is not an option," he retorted. "Everybody out."

I sat up. "Are you nuts? I'm not going." I knew that it was a mistake to put water in the gasoline tanks. Part of our job was to drain all the tanks daily to keep the water level below the pump-out line. If water was put in, then water would be pumped out along with the gasoline, causing plane crashes because excess water in the gasoline would not allow the plane engines to function.

He insisted. "You are refusing an order. You could be court-martialed."

I jumped up, livid that they hadn't considered the consequences of their plan of action. "Court-martialed for refusing to help the enemy? You guys are crazy. All right, go ahead! Court-martial! I demand an immediate court-martial. I want to find out whose side you nuts are on, and get the damn adjutant general here to straighten out who the hell we're fighting for."

Poor Sergeant Benes. He was so taken aback, he went outside the grass hut that we called home and talked to someone. All I heard was mumbling. He came back in and insisted, "Everybody out."

I had not yet gotten them to take me seriously. Desperate, I said, "No. Let's get this damn court-martial under way before you screw up the Philippine invasion." He did not back down. I reverted to sarcasm. "Water comes in with the gasoline from the ships. You don't need to put water in. Just drain them less often till the planes begin crashing, and then you can start draining again."

The sergeant went out again. This time I heard, "Does he know what he is talking about?"

"I think so, sir," someone said. "He's the one we sent to Tulsa who's supposed to know more about it than anyone else we have. He is very definite and determined."

"All right, let's go see Lieutenant Greenthal about this guy." I had already clashed with Lieutenant Greenthal, the executive officer, on the trip to New Guinea on board ship; he did not have a favorable impression of me.

About fifteen minutes later, we received the order that everyone was to go out to play volleyball. Everybody played about a half hour, then rested a half hour, on and off for most of the day; yet I, who had been on night duty, was left on the court playing, or at least acting like I was playing while I stood, dog-tired, the whole morning and afternoon. However, no pipeline was ever laid for water supply to the gasoline storage holding tanks, so no water was ever added to contaminate the gasoline going to the aircraft carriers. Our planes were safe; so was the need for obedience in the military, as I was publicly corrected for challenging an order.

I saw Lieutenant Greenthal again later in the war in Japan, after I had been transferred out of his unit to work in the lab. For some reason, he himself brought the samples for testing to the lab, saying he had to see Captain So-and-so and thought he would stop by and see how I was doing—as if we were friends! Me, an Italian from California, and him, a Jew from New York.

I think he realized that despite our confrontations, I really was interested in making the army the best it could be. Because I had felt powerless, I used a tactic I hoped would get immediate attention and stop the action I knew to be incorrect.

## *Moving On When Not Appreciated*

Our work is a major part of our lives, so it is important that we feel fairly compensated for it. Negotiating for a higher salary or wage is an option more often than one would think, since the employees' experience, education, and ideas for the business do differ. Many people are unschooled in such negotiation; consider it a form of assertiveness in that you are standing up for yourself.

After serving in the war, I went back to school, graduated from the University of California at Berkeley with a degree in chemical engineering, and married Ileane a year later. Within seven years of our marriage, when I had a wife and four children to support, I had a critical decision to make about staying in a job that was safe but did not recognize my very evident contributions, or risk the move to yet another company. Here is the story.

When I worked at Stauffer Chemical in Richmond, California, in 1956, I was promoted to Superphosphate Plant Superintendent. Phosphate is the main ingredient in any solid fertilizer. Our phosphate came by train from Wyoming, in a boxcar. I noticed a way we could improve the unloading system. What they were doing to get it out of the train cars and to its site on our plant was a very slow, labor-intensive method. An operator with a front-end loader would drive up a ramp, go into the car, pick up a load, back out, and dump it into a hopper car, over and over again. Forty thousand tons of powdered phosphate rock, almost like flour in its powdered form, all unloaded very inefficiently. One could expect a loss of one percent because it was a powder that flew into the air. But since our method of transfer exposed it so much, losses always exceeded one percent, as over four hundred tons were released over the plant and environs annually.

I drew up my plan and submitted it to the engineering department so we could upgrade the process from "scoop and dump" to a conveyor system. It would require a concrete pit to be built under the railroad track, into which the phosphate would be unloaded. From the pit, underground, a screw conveyor in a twenty-inch tube would take the phosphate powder to the waiting hopper car. (The phosphate would have to come from Wyoming in a hopper car instead of a boxcar, but that actually would cost less.) No loss of powder would occur, since the path from the railroad to our own site was all underground. The phosphate was being moved forward in a tube by a constantly revolving corkscrew.

The construction estimate for the job from our engineering department was about four times higher than I imagined. I could not believe it had to be that expensive, so I went to a conveyor designer on my own time and presented him with my problem. His initial reaction was "Nothing to it; simple as all get-out." His total price for everything except installation (and he offered to show us how to do that) was one-eighth the engineering department's estimate.

With that information, I used the hierarchy principle and talked to the plant manager, suggesting that the maintenance superintendent and I would do the job rather than Engineering. Just to be on the safe side, I doubled the consultant's estimated cost, which still made it one fourth of the engineering estimate. Jack Edwards, the plant manager, made a couple of phone calls, then told me to go ahead. At that point, I told the maintenance superintendent about the deal; he was enthusiastic because he was going to show up the division engineering department.

The conveyor was completed under budget, and it worked like a charm. The unloading rate increased from 100 tons per shift to 225 tons per shift, so we never again needed a second shift, resulting in wage savings for the company. Losses of the phosphate at our plant dropped to zero, equaling more savings. Considering the environmental and financial benefit to the company (I estimated that this saved over $50,000 annually), I expected some kind of appropriate reward, either a raise or a substantial bonus.

On my next paycheck at annual review time, I received an increase of thirty dollars a month; the company (union members) received an increase of thirty-one dollars and fifty cents per month. I could not believe it! They were giving me three hundred and sixty dollars for the year's raise when my initiative saved them fifty thousand. This was less than a one percent raise. Even more insulting, the company union people who provided labor but little design or initiative received more of a raise than I did.

The next morning I immediately went to see the plant manager and explained what I perceived to be a great inequity. He did not promise a thing in response. I felt completely unappreciated, but did not leave; I bided my time. I didn't know what I would do, but I knew I would make some change.

About four months later, another opportunity for reward passed me by. The research and development department received a twenty-five dollar per month cost-of-living raise. In manufacturing, we received nothing. I felt really angry at the injustice again, but I could not go to the plant manager that afternoon; I needed to visit my mother, who was in Alta Bates Hospital in Oakland.

At the hospital, I was delayed in seeing her for some reason. As I sat in the hospital lobby, cooling my heels, I noticed a public phone across the hall and decided to call Dow Chemical in Pittsburg, California, which was only ten miles from my house. Perhaps they had an opening for a chemical engineer. The personnel assistant was very interested in my qualifications, took my information, and sent me an application for employment. I filled it out and mailed it in. About two weeks later I had an interview at the Dow Pittsburg Plant. It was very heartening.

I decided to give my notice to Stauffer when Dow made me a starting salary offer fifteen percent higher than my salary at Stauffer. At that point, another option would have been to let Stauffer know what Dow was willing to pay me and give Stauffer an opportunity to match or beat it. I chose to go to Dow; I had no confidence that Stauffer would recognize initiative and excellence in the future if they had not done so now.

On my last day at Stauffer, the personnel manager from New York had a meeting with me, asking why I would leave a job in which I was obviously doing very well. I told him bluntly, "You are not paying me enough." He did not offer more or try to keep me on. Perhaps he was not authorized to do so.

Some people might respond to the lack of raises or bonuses by deciding to cease innovating and keep their ideas for improving the system to themselves. Others might try to make their point to management by working very slowly on purpose, or not reporting supply needs or maintenance requests in a timely manner. These tactics do no one any good. If straightforward discussion about what you have given the company does not work, consider which other businesses might need and value your skills more than this one. I felt strongly about using my talents and ideas for the betterment of the company, rather than staying and complaining or trying to get back at Stauffer. I chose to look elsewhere, refusing to stay where I knew my initiative was not going to be rewarded adequately and fairly.

Standing up for oneself can be a split-second decision or a well-considered process. In either case, it is important to use the assertiveness or aggressiveness that is appropriate for the situation. When my grandfather had no police support, he decided to take the law into his own hands, but he did it only after giving a warning, in order to enforce the rules his community supported. He did not use his power in random lawlessness, to beat up people for the fun of it, nor to threaten for extortion as did the Mafia.

When my father and I left the jobs we considered to be out of step with our values, we did so only after trying to influence the decision-makers to meet our needs; then we made other arrangements to provide for our families. Being assertive is not a license to disregard the needs of one's dependents.

My young mother felt responsible for my welfare, which gave her the courage to withstand her husband and her intimidating father-in-law (with the backing of her mother) so that I might be cared for wisely. In her case, the intensity of her feelings gave her courage, and her mother supported her with the advice to negotiate. She gained power because of that act of assertiveness.

On the other hand, my brother stood up for himself to make a point about being respected within his own family. His was a situation of the last straw, not being willing to tolerate any more disrespect. He suffered by having to walk eight miles that day to get home; but his rebellion was effective, and he was not subjected to criticism and disrespect like that again.

It is necessary to balance one's needs and those of others. Use assertiveness for the purpose of creating order and contributing to family and society. Be certain all other options are exhausted before resorting to the tactic of aggression. With proper consideration of the type of behavior needed to get through to the person or persons you want to influence, assertiveness will ultimately lead to success.

# Chapter Three: Act with Charity and Integrity

The way people behave in daily life, under routine circumstances, forms their character. Qualities such as charity (giving without expecting in return) and integrity (doing the right thing even when no one else knows) become part of a person's character through small decisions that might not seem very important.

Both of these traits are very important for immigrants. Having an attitude of giving without expecting something in return fosters a cooperative spirit, an openness to your new country, and brings out a similar spirit in others. The ones to whom you give need not be poor people, just those who have a momentary need that you can meet with your skills or tools, often without much sacrifice on your part. Acting with integrity builds a solid reputation among your new acquaintances and business contacts. Each time you decide to be generous, honest, or courageous and act with integrity, you build a framework of good character that makes it easier for you to choose similar good behaviors in the future, and it makes you a person whom other immigrants and present citizens are willing to trust. Some might think that watching out for oneself at all costs is the most important value, but such an attitude will be self-defeating. This chapter shares stories that show the effects of a decision based on the values of charity and integrity.

## A Good Reputation Is Security

The first time my grandfather John came to the United States, he was alone and did not know the language, and his goal was to save as much money as possible to send back home to Marutza, his wife. But he resisted the temptation to overcharge and gain extra money quickly, which probably saved his life.

John joined other Italians in St. Louis, working as a fruit and vegetable peddler going from house to house. He regularly attended to the needs of the well-to-do in the St. Louis "Hill" area, charging a fair price and serving his customers with a pleasant attitude. If he thought about overcharging these customers for the produce because they had much money, he did not do so. His reputation thus formed as a person who was honest and conscientious.

Late one autumn, while he was working, a blizzard hit suddenly. He had not dressed for it and got drenched. Then, before he could leave the area, the freeze came, and he was stuck, miles from his home. Of course, no public transportation was able to move; everything was iced in. He approached his final customer, but he was in a pitiful condition. Fortunately, it was a home at which he had sold fruits and vegetables for several years. The lady of the house knew him as honest and trustworthy and insisted that he remain there overnight, even though her husband was not at home. She even promised that her husband would take him home the next day. However, John developed chills and fever that were so severe that the lady got him into bed and dried his clothes. Her husband, returning very late, was informed of John's condition. The couple insisted that he stay with them until he got well. It turned out to be nearly a week. Then they took him back to his home in their carriage and gave him clothes that the husband felt John could use.

John remembered their kindness all his life, but it would not have been offered had he not been known as trustworthy or deemed as trustworthy because of his business interactions with them. That was their only opportunity to get a sense of this quality in him.

## *Charles, the Jew*

My father was born in Sicily, when Grandfather John went back after years in St. Louis. Thus, my father had to apply for citizenship here in the United States. He did so when I was in the sixth grade. For the application, Dad had to have a middle name, but had not been given one at birth. He took the name Charles. This is why.

When Dad himself was about twelve years old, an elderly Jewish man came into the Italian community at Martinez to sell clothes. Since most of the adults did not speak English, this man was at a loss. When my father piped up and offered to help him by translating, Charles asked, "How much?" Dad responded that he did not want any money; he'd just like to help. Perhaps it made the boy feel needed and important; perhaps he felt some sense of responsibility to help out an elder at a disadvantage. Maybe he was remembering how his own father needed help in communicating with the English-speaking world; he was very likely doing what had been modeled to him in the family: help others when you can. In any case, Dad made the offer out of charity, and Charles took him up on it. They became fast friends.

As time went on, Charles taught Dad about business. Over the course of several years, he paid Dad more money than Dad would have ever thought to ask for, and gave Dad clothes that were in the right style. Dad for his part was always there to help Charles, saving him time and enabling him to get more sales with the advice to come to town after the fishing seasons ended, when money was plentiful. A generation of years later at my father's citizenship ceremony, this mentoring relationship, based on charity by both parties, was still so precious to him that he chose to take Charles's name for his own. Isn't it a sign of a new culture forming when a name in an Italian Bellecci clan comes from a Jewish clothes peddler?

## *The Chatterbox Meets His Match*

Part of integrity is respect for all people. Children need to be taught respect for elders, even those of different cultures. One of my lessons in this trait occurred in a situation with our next-door neighbors, the Davis couple. They rented the house from my grandfather (who, by the way, continued the custom of saving and buying property in the United States, borrowing $1,000 at ten percent interest from the Bank of Italy to purchase it). Mrs. Davis liked me to visit her because she had no children yet, and I was someone to whom she could talk. However, at times I became tired of her (to me) idle chatter, and I would tell her to be quiet in the Sicilian dialect. To her it sounded like I was saying "teetee" when in reality I was saying, "*Tzee-thee,*" Sicilian for "shut up."

When she found out after several weeks what I was saying, she chased me around the yard, caught me, and gave me a big hug, but told me, "No more teetees." I'm sure my parents reinforced the need for this respect.

## *No Cost, No Charge*

This story illustrates the concept of charity toward someone we might not normally consider in need of "charity." However, giving to those in need does not always mean financial need, though an act of charity might be worth a great deal in the long run.

In 1947, while I was back at college after the war, a contractor named Charlie Murietti was building just around the block from my mom and dad's house. Dad noticed one day that Charlie's machine had stopped and went to see why. Charlie said he needed a part and had to send off for a new one, lamenting that it would be weeks before it came in. Dad was a precision machinist; he told Charlie he could fix it in one day. He took the part to work the next day, fixed it on his own time, and returned it to Charlie in good order. Charlie was amazed. Thanks to Dad's attitude of being of service, instead of being unable to continue work for several weeks, Charlie had only lost twenty-four hours. This was during a construction boom after World War II, when contractors could not put up buildings fast enough.

Dad did not charge Charlie anything because he said it did not cost him anything to do it. Charlie was eternally grateful and showed his gratitude by stopping what he was doing anytime one of us came to his office with a building need, which was somewhat often as we built houses for my family, my sisters Marie and Rosalie, and for my brother Frank. Charlie also showed us a way to properly attach a sub floor to a concrete foundation, and often bought truckloads of lumber for us at his wholesale price, not charging us anything over his cost. Dad did not expect this kind of repayment, but had the attitude of old-fashioned neighborliness, doing all the good he could in any way that he could.

Dad was well known for his habit of charity. He was always doing work for free, going and coming at all hours to help people by working on their car and boat engines (there were no repair shops in those days) or taking them out fishing. My mother sometimes became perturbed, however, as he often missed the dinner hour but still wanted his food to be hot and ready whenever he walked in. (Recall that we had no microwave ovens in those days, and no cell phones to alert one another.) To express their gratitude, the people Dad helped would bring fruits or vegetables or meats, which Mom always accepted graciously.

The family still laughs, though, about how she handled one item she could never appreciate, which was mustard greens. My brother Frank's godfather, Paul Ventimiglia (which means "twenty miles"), brought greens over often. Mom was very gracious, smiling and telling him thank you, and then she would throw it in the trash as soon as he left. She said she did not want to embarrass him by telling him we did not eat it, but she also complained to my father, "We take him fishing; he brings us grass. What are we supposed to do with grass?"

In any case, Dad's habit of giving his skills and talents for the good of others expanded the Bellecci reputation of being a family one could count on. Whereas Grandfather John gave of himself in leadership, courage, and honesty, Dad had the same traits, but usually gave of his talents. People who needed help but could not pay money still had a chance to get their needs met. Dad believed that helping someone else would eventually help us all succeed.

# *Help without Taking Advantage*

A few years later, I was married, working, building our house, and losing sleep because we had a toddler and an infant. I had the opportunity to help without counting the cost, as my family did before me. Unfortunately, because I was so tired, I balked at first, but in the end, I did what I knew was the right thing to do.

The winter of 1951 was very wet in Concord, California. The area in which we built our house did not have a paved road for the last mile. One night, coming home late from work, I parked the car at the corner of the paved road and walked the distance to our home. Once I arrived, my wife Ileane informed me that some boys in a car were stuck on the road near our house. We housed one of my sister's Fordson tractors in the garage so I could pull my car through the muck, if necessary; thus, I could always count on being able to get to work. I knew she was aware I could use that for these boys.

Reluctantly, already tired from my long day, I got out the tractor and pulled the boys' car to the paved road. It was the right thing to do. How could I go into my house and relax when they were stuck, and I could have done something to help? My father and grandfather had often left the comfort of their homes to help others. By the time I finished with the boys' car, three other cars had gotten stuck. I pulled them all to the paved section as well, looking forward to some food and dry clothes very soon.

Then I saw one more car about a hundred yards away from the paved road. The driver came running to ask for help. I was tired, wet, and hungry and told him to call AAA. He said he had already tried, but they had refused him. He offered to pay whatever I wanted. Tired as I was, I refused to take any money and went ahead and pulled him out too. Though I could have made a good deal of money for my services for all of the cars, I did not think it was fair to charge them when they were just as annoyed with the whole situation as I was. In a few more minutes, I was in dry clothes and had eaten and could relax with my family. Everyone who had been stuck was relieved and had gone on with their evening. I did not regret helping.

As things turned out, about six months later we received an enormous bill of $1,350 from the electric company for the extra length of utility lines we needed. We were the first house built on that road, and Pacific Gas and Electric had to lay lines for nearly half a mile to our house. Eventually, other homes were built which also used those lines.

At that time, we had no money to pay that bill and could not foresee doing so since I was making only $400 a month. With this huge bill in hand,

I went to the PG&E office in Concord. As I was explaining the situation, a manager came out of the back office. He asked if I was the one who had pulled him out of the mud last winter but refused any payment. I was surprised that he asked, since when I did the favor, it was dark, and neither of us could see the other clearly. But he said he remembered my voice, which he described as "very distinct." He tore up the bill and said to bring him any others I might get. We never got any other bills for the extra utility lines.

Not every good deed comes back like that, but even if it had not, I felt satisfied in knowing I had acted with integrity, had been charitable with the use of the tractor, and had done the right thing. In the next story, my brother Frank got a turn to use the resources and power he had to act with charity and do what was right.

## *Ignore Ridicule*

When my brother Frank attended City College in San Francisco, he took a course in hotel and restaurant management. For experience, he worked as night manager at a restaurant in the area. He noticed each night that the extra food was getting thrown out, and he mentioned it to some friends. One of those friends knew that some of the college's black football players had limited money to eat and ravenous appetites. He asked Frank about helping them out by letting them have that extra food. Frank agreed it was a great idea and told him to have them come in at the tail end of the restaurant's hours.

The football players did come in several times a week, and they were given free meals from the food that would have been wasted. They were grateful, but Frank treated them not as "charity cases" but as people who were doing him a favor. They all enjoyed talking about football and other sports. Frank remembers that Ollie Matson was one of the players who came in regularly. He was a future all-pro player in the National Football League.

Not many years later, Frank went into surveying, working for Contra Costa County. He was soon promoted to Surveyor Party Chief due to his excellent work ethic and his trustworthy measuring skills. In the 1960s, racial issues between blacks and whites in the United States were very sensitive due to emerging civil rights activities making people aware of long-term prejudice. When the county hired two black men, Frank immediately took one man on his crew, but no one was willing to accept the other. Prejudice and stereotyping ran too deep.

Frank's previous experiences in getting to know the black football players led him to accept both men, noting, "I don't care what color they are, as long as they can do the work!" Other men in Frank's department and some of those outside the department, but employed by the county, ridiculed Frank. Even those who were Frank's chums in high school now ridiculed him to his face, unmistakably and quite rudely, about the new black crew workers. I am fairly certain that their mean-spirited words and actions hurt Frank deeply. Frank never responded with insult, however.

Frank and his crew continued to do precision work, which was no small task since surveying for concrete was required to be within one-sixteenth of an inch on a roadway. One of the two new hires became a licensed surveyor, a perfectionist in his own right. The other worked his way up in the union, becoming one of its leaders. Frank, for his part, carried on the Bellecci reputation, the third generation living in the town of Martinez to do what was right, choosing to act with integrity in spite of very negative social pressure.

## Be Consistent with Requirements

If you want to succeed, whether in business, in parenting, in teaching, or socially, it is important to be consistent in the standards you expect of everyone and to let others know your expectations. Though you might be tempted to let friends or favorites get by, or let those who seem to have connections do less than expected, if you treat everyone alike, you will be able to defend your actions, and those around you will have better morale. When policies are in writing, it helps you stick with them.

In 1974, I was plant manager at Borden Chemical in Baton Rouge, Louisiana. We received a letter from the Equal Employment Opportunity Commission (EEOC) stating that we had racially discriminated against a black woman and that the New Orleans office director would be contacting us. He very soon did, saying that if we rehired the woman, all would be forgiven; otherwise, he would have to charge us with unfair labor practices. Before responding, I reviewed the case with our personnel manager, J.T. Jennings, and with the supervisor involved.

According to our records, she had worked well for about three months, the probationary period, but once that was over, she decided she was above the rules. Since we had a chemical plant with many hazards, it was critical that she follow the safety rules and other guidelines, just like everyone else. She had been given reviews and a chance to correct her unsafe habits but had not. Her behavior had put herself and other workers in danger; she had not given her best so the products we made could be the best. It was not discrimination; I decided to fight the charge.

Taking on a government agency for a racial issue at that time almost felt like David going against Goliath. I called the Corporate Personnel VP at Borden's headquarters in Columbus, Ohio, to let them know what we were telling EEOC: we were not taking her back. She had been treated more than fairly. The case was well documented. I also told the people at headquarters that, if we lost this one, we should go out of business, because we would never be able to make a firing stick; our workforce would know they could all break the rules as she had.

J.T. informed the EEOC Director of the decision; he responded by coming to the plant with the discharged employee. He stated his surprise that our plant had no record of any EEOC charges, but warned he would have to file a complaint if we did not rehire her. J.T. gave the director some background on our type of business, the dangers involved, the training periods and reviews by at least two supervisors on a continuing basis for three years. Failure along the way was reason for discharge. We informed the director that we did not hire lightly, and we did not fire lightly. We tried very much to have our hires succeed. We intended to fight this in court as far as we needed to go and planned to publicize its unfairness. That got his attention.

He then proposed to forget the whole thing, get rid of all the paperwork in his office if we would list her as resigned for personal reasons. We were skeptical, asking, "How would we know that would be done?"

He replied that everything went to Washington, D.C., and since he had not sent anything yet, nothing *would* be sent, and there would be no records of anything in his office. We told him that, after we checked out his story, we would complete the agreement on our end. As he left, he said, "You know, she is pregnant, and in a couple months she wouldn't be able to work anyway." We had not known, but stated we were sorry she chose not to be a regular employee. His story checked out, and we completed the agreement.

The willingness to stand up to the government agency was seen by some in the company as foolish or of no avail. I believed we had to do so for several reasons, besides the fact that it was the right thing to do. We knew the rest of the employees, black and white, were aware of the poor work record of the one we had fired and that she did not deserve to be rehired. For the sake of future productivity and discipline, we felt it was imperative that we fight it.

Immigrants who work as employees, who are parents, or who teach in any capacity or volunteer—all will encounter a situation when they know they must take a stand, or their rules will mean nothing to anyone. Take courage, and be assertive.

# *Focus on the Issue, and Make a Decision*

In 1976, I was new to the board of directors of the Louisiana Chemical Association (LCA). Sometimes a new person has a fresh perspective that more involved members will need. But speaking up when you are new takes the courage of integrity, of doing what is right, no matter what.

The board was to select a paid executive to administer the Association business, to represent us at the State Capitol on issues involving the chemical industry, and to lobby when necessary, as well as run the office. A search process netted three final candidates, of whom I knew none. I listened to other board members hash and rehash the same facts without coming to an answer, because none of the candidates were perfect.

I finally said, "Look, you really only have one choice. Going over this same stuff isn't going to change anything. I move we vote. If none of them gets a majority, then we have to look further." The board agreed. The one selected was one who could grow into the job, with guidance from the board.

The meetings were supposed to be confidential, but in an ironic twist, the word got around that I had made a strong push for the one elected, and others went along with me because I wanted him in the job. It was completely untrue. In spite of this false laying of responsibility, I would make the same suggestion if I had to do it over, because I could tell the board was stuck, and I could see why. When you are the person with a fresh perspective, it is like having the skill or tool that is needed for a job, as my father and grandfather had, even if it is not a tool you hold in your hands.

Almost ten years later, when I was a member of the same board again, the same type of opportunity to help came up again. In 1986, the discussion of the LCA board related to the director selected ten years prior. The problem was that this director had not been satisfactory through at least the terms of three presidents (between three and six years, total), and a decision for or against termination was needed. Again, I listened to hours of discussion as to why he had to go, but no one would call for a vote, nor was anyone willing to go the necessary step of moving to terminate.

Finally I asked, "Has anyone here ever fired anyone too soon? My problem with every termination has been that it was overdue. The people should have been canned sooner than I finally canned them. You are saying that this termination should have occurred years ago, is that correct?" To a man, they said yes. "Well, what are we waiting for? Is there any real reason for further discussion?" No, they stated. So we all voted. Later on, word leaked out that I was the one who had the executive fired. Some things never change.

In spite of being blamed while innocent, for a third time I interacted with this board, again speaking up to identify the true problem. Perhaps it was necessary again because people will purposely continue nonproductive discussion when they are afraid of taking responsibility for making a decision. On this board, where confidentiality seemed nonexistent, it was understandable.

Still, I was again surprised by the need to focus the discussion and felt exasperated at the lengthy debate. The new director believed the board needed a person with expertise to refute at the Capitol the unsubstantiated allegations of some well-meaning but uninformed environmentalists. The discussion got sidetracked, however, as to whether these representatives of the companies and managers of chemical plants up and down the Mississippi River had the authority to obligate their company to the added expense of the additional staff person. I finally stood up and, somewhat forcefully, asked: "Do we need the person? Whether any of our managements agrees to the added cost is not the problem. If they don't agree, we shall have to drop out of the LCA; if they do agree, we stay in. The point is: do we need this environmental person on the LCA staff?" I moved for a vote, which turned out forty-nine to one in favor of the added person.

It seems that this group of leaders was waiting for a person to facilitate their decision-making. Because of the habit cultivated in my family about speaking up for what is right, I did it. I never knew my grandfather or father to regret a situation in which they did so, even if the consequence was more severe than the blame that I received. Doing right will bring a sense of satisfaction and self-affirmation that is independent of what others think of you.

## *Dishonesty Ultimately Does Not Pay*

Opportunities for stealing abound in a workplace, in a neighborhood, in retail stores, everywhere. But besides being against the law, stealing is not the recommended behavior for a person who wants to be a success in this country. Trying to bypass rules, to charge too much, to overcomplicate the job so you can charge more, or to take the shortest way to solve a problem might seem to be clever and help you get rich quickly. I've seen that the quick and dishonest way usually ends up costing more than one thinks.

Recently, Ileane and I learned that our extension ladder was stolen from a building we own in Louisiana. The lock had been cut off and the chain tossed onto the roof; it was quite deliberate. When we needed an air-conditioner repair at that building, I alerted the repairman that he would now need to bring his own ladder to get to the AC units on the roof. After he completed the job, he asked what I planned to do about a ladder. I told him, "I don't know what I'm going to do, but I hope the guy who took it doesn't get hurt."

One of the men standing with us asked, "Why do you say that?"

"Well, because anytime somebody steals something, it comes back to bite him."

"Yeah, I guess you're right."

"Oh, I know I'm right. You don't know *how* it will go badly, but it usually does. Maybe it's because they didn't learn how to use the stolen item safely, so they get hurt, or they break it. Or, since they didn't pay for it, they don't have the motivation to take care of it correctly, and the item rusts or goes bad quickly, so no one gets to use it. Or maybe it happens that those who steal usually keep company with others who do the same and then have items stolen from them. Something always goes wrong; stealing does not help people get ahead."

Over the years, I have had experiences go both ways, for me and against me. The pattern has been clear, and it is easy to see for anyone who wants to pay attention to it.

Integrity knows no national boundaries, no race, no gender. All people who make a habit of acting with integrity in matters large and small, not taking the convenient route or the easy way out but doing what is right or charitable, will find that habit keeps them steady on their road to success. Sometimes family and friends provide support for necessary courage, but there will be times when one's colleagues and friends will disappoint, as with my brother Frank's friends or my management peers. When joining a new society, the habits of charity and integrity rank among the most important values to practice.

# Chapter Four: Expect Excellence, and Put Forth the Effort

Excellence can be fostered by almost any person involved in one's life. Parents can expect, role models can demonstrate, teachers can encourage, co-workers can support, and supervisors can reward. The sooner excellence is expected and supported, the more likely it is that a person will use his or her full potential on a daily, consistent basis. One must put forth this kind of good, consistent effort in order to achieve excellence.

It was no secret that excellence was expected in all facets in our family. Sometimes the fervor with which we approached our tasks could be alarming, as this first story indicates.

Once when I was back from the war and had registered for college, but before the semester started, my father was remodeling a house in the daytime and fishing at night. He required me to help at both. One of my cousins, whose father was also going fishing at night, knew it should be rest time during the day. She knew of my father's reputation, since his youth, for being extremely intense and a perfectionist about any job that he did. My cousin asked my mother, "When Johnny works and does things, is he like his father?" I think she was wondering if there could possibly be two like that in one family!

Mom replied, "Not as much."

## *My Go-Getter Grandmother*

I have been surprised when I witness people accepting mediocrity. In my experiences, no one in charge of me let it happen. I was surrounded by excellence and by hard workers. My maternal grandmother Marianna (or Marian) Russo, "Ma" (the name by which I called her, which came to be used by the rest of the clan), was amazing. She moved to the United States as the new bride of Antonio Russo, wound up in Black Diamond, California, and set about making the best of what she considered a bad lot. Marianna had two miscarriages before my mother was born in 1906. Then five more children followed. Unfortunately, she had to endure the grief of losing still another of her children, a boy who died from an accident with firecrackers. The surviving children were my mother Mary, Uncle Joe, Uncle Salvador (whom we called Uncle Dutchie), Aunt Catherine (Katie), and Uncle Frank; all born in Black Diamond. Due to lots of prayers, her fortitude and her attitude of embracing the hard work involved in doing three different sideline jobs, Marianna cared for her family, kept them together, and eventually was quite successful. How she did this is described in the stories that follow.

In a pattern similar to that of Grandfather John sending money back home, one of Marianna's jobs directly benefited her sisters back home in the town of Palermo, Sicily. During the ten or so years between her arrival and World War I, while birthing and raising children and keeping house, Marianna arranged to accept jewelry sent from her sisters in Sicily to sell to the women and men of the Italian communities in Pittsburg and Martinez. She would rebate to her sisters a share of the profits. She conducted that business until the shipping was stopped between the two countries due to the First World War.

My parents' marriage came about due to Marianna's willingness to work hard. Her uncle was my grandfather John Bellecci. She always visited John when in Martinez to sell jewelry, and having similar outgoing, hardworking natures, with the values outlined in this book, they became very good friends. John's daughter, Dad's oldest sister, Marian Aiello, became a lifelong close friend of Marianna Russo; both had been named to respect Marianna Flores, a family ancestor. My dad came to know Marianna's oldest daughter, Mary, whom he later married, thanks to this working connection which turned into friendship.

In between bearing children, Marianna would also work at the local cannery during its busy summer and fall seasons. She was so good with people, disputes, and efficient work that even my demanding father praised her by saying, "She would have been a forelady if she knew English." (She never did learn it.) Her supplements to the family income were welcome. When she wasn't working at the cannery, she saved money by making her husband's oilcloth rainwear for fishing.

The fishermen who went out with Grandfather Tony were envious of the protective clothes that he had, which they could not get anywhere. Learning that his wife made those rain- and water-protective clothes, they prevailed on her to outfit them. She agreed, but charged a fair price. She would sew the jackets, trousers, hoods, and aprons, and then dip them in raw linseed oil. The muslin cloth that she used was the highest quality and the strongest cloth that she could find, purchased in San Francisco. The dipping and draining of the raw linseed oil were repeated several times with a drying period after each dipping and draining. She used raw linseed oil because the boiled would harden in time while the raw stayed flexible indefinitely. For years my grandmother continued in that business, until after World War II.

Ma was always busy doing something. My mother would say, "She's made of iron." She was a big help to my mother, who had a difficult time with each of her five pregnancies. My father and Marianna remained fast friends throughout her life, as noted in her very diplomatic handling of the situation when I was six months old and drunk on brandied fruit. Theirs was the antithesis of the typical mother-in-law / son-in-law relationship.

## *Take Work Where You Find It*

Seasonal work is a critical income producer for families in newcomer or marginal living conditions. In California at that time, seasonal work was available from early June through late September by picking fruit and vegetables, and fishing, and in the fall as well one had the opportunity to harvest grapes in the vineyards.

To get out of the marginal income bracket, people aiming to be a success need to take advantage of work when it comes up or where they can find it. In the U.S. today, extra income might be had by doubling up in jobs by doing seasonal farm work, as we did, or in retail stores or mail delivery during Christmas time, and the like. Home hobbies or crafts might also be turned into extra money for mothers with young children, like my grandmother. I suggest these because I saw it work so well in my family.

The extra money we made was not spent on "keeping up with the Joneses"; that is, buying the latest convenience or most expensive version of an item. Rather, the money was saved to invest in property. In fact, in the early days, someone from the Italian community who bought a Cadillac instead of a Ford was considered stupid for throwing away so much money that could have been invested wisely.

In the present time, I have noticed that parents will work seasonally to earn extra money to buy their children name-brand clothes and shoes, expensive video gaming equipment, and the latest in technology; they buy themselves fancy cars, many clothes, and big-screen or plasma TVs. These are luxury items that all break or are outgrown.

Land does not depreciate or decay. Investing in land and working to own one's home is a much wiser use of extra income, if a family wants to truly be financially independent in this country. Due to intense and constant marketing and advertising, it is probably harder today to resist getting the children the many status symbols, but wise parents will resist and invest in the future.

## *Intense Work Pays Off*

The men in my family also believed in taking work when and where it presented itself, and seasonal work played a prominent role in their success. My grandfathers were commercial fishermen, and they worked incredibly hard each year during the four to six weeks of intense fishing in spring and in fall. The hours to fish were round the clock, from dusk Sunday evening till dawn on the next Saturday morning. The thirty-six hour pause from Saturday to Sunday was due to the U.S. Fish and Game law, to make sure that some salmon or other fish actually made it to the spawning grounds. The schedule the fishermen kept was this: out on the boat till a full catch, come into the dock, unload the fish, and go back on the water, round the clock, catching as many of the tides as they could. After "laying out a drift" (laying the nets across an expanse of water), one partner would watch the boat while the other slept for forty-five minutes or an hour; then they'd haul in the fish, move the boat to the next area, lay out the nets again, and the other partner would get in a nap on that drift.

This hauling in of the nets required tremendous shoulder and arm strength, as the nets were 200 fathoms long (that's 1,200 feet) and were pulled up hand over hand. They were even heavier due to being soaking wet with the salt water and, hopefully, laden with salmon in the fall and shad in the spring. Two men worked in each boat. They brought a lunch box full of food; when unloading fish at the dock, they could buy a loaf of bread and lunch meat. Sometimes Grandfather used a little charcoal grill in the boat and would barbecue a fish. Keeping up that kind of intensity for those weeks and getting the best and most fish earned Grandfather John the reputation of Number One Fisherman. ("Giovanni, Numero Uno!" the others would say when they referred to him.)

I worked in the boats when home. I personally know the intensity and strength required and had an unsought opportunity to show it. In the fall of 1946, I went back to college one week late because of helping with the salmon fishing. Government regulations required a PE class, and one of the few classes left with openings was a body-building class. My friend from Frosh baseball and I signed up. The rest of the class looked like they needed a body-building class; the two of us were athletic and in excellent physical condition.

In our first class the instructor wanted to show us all what poor shape we were in, so he told us climb directly up a twenty-foot rope hanging from the ceiling. As a "B" alphabetically, I was about fourth or fifth in line. None of the previous students even got halfway. I suggested he call on me last because I would blow the deal for him. He would not listen to me. "OK," I said. After six weeks of pulling two hundred fathoms of forty mesh net soaked with salty water, my hands were like leather; my arms could lift triple the weight that I was at that time (something under two hundred pounds). I shot up the rope and slid down without so much as a deep breath. The class clapped, and he told me to see him after class. He wanted to know how I could possibly have developed so much arm strength. I told him about the fishing. He wanted to know how many one-armed pushups I could do. After twenty, I just stopped. He then gripped my hand and was further impressed. But such physical strength was common among the fishermen.

The money earned from their intense schedule during the spring and fall could get them about half a year's income, but it would not last all year. However, Alaska's fishing season was seven days a week for six weeks. (It was not a state in the Union then and did not have to abide by the thirty-six hour "pause" rule.) With that length of time available to fish, a family had income for the whole year. In order to make more money, my Grandfather John would sometimes fish there and in San Pedro as well as the Carquinez Straits. Another option was going to Monterey for ocean fishing. In ocean fishing, they would use baited hooks on half a dozen bamboo "arms" which fanned out around the boat, watched over by the men.

The physical feat of fishing required preparation and perseverance, both qualities necessary for excellence. It does not just happen by chance or by wanting to do it. A fisherman and his family had to prepare and be ready and willing to make the sacrifices necessary for it. The fishermen were willing and proved such excellence. In the town of Martinez today, mounted beside the wharf where the fishermen used to dock their boats and repair their nets, a plaque names and commemorates the incredible efforts of my grandfather John and the many other fishermen of the Italian community.

## *Expectations Start Early*

When I was young, we lived on Escobar Street, a block and a half from the county courthouse and a block away from a Piggly-Wiggly grocery store, at the corner of Main and Las Juntas streets. When I was five years old, my mother began sending me to the store with a note and exact change to the penny. She had two more even younger children at home; I was expected to help out. Just a few months later, still no older than five, she sent me to the store without a note. I was supposed to remember what it was she needed. The trips to the store occurred almost every day because in 1928, we did not have a refrigerator; nobody did. Of course, if I made an error, I was sent right back to the store to correct it. I made a lot of trips to Piggly-Wiggly. Eventually, I'm sure, I learned to get it right the first time.

## *Don't Be a "Lanyusso"*

Height has its advantages and disadvantages. Because I was tall, when I was twelve, my grandmother Ma insisted I join the fourteen- to sixteen-year-olds who were spending their summer picking apricots (in June), peaches (July), and pears (later in the summer and early fall). There was no way I could explain to my grandmother that these boys were all two years older than I; nor could I convince her that I was still a kid who deserved to play a few more years. No. My father had been put to work at the age of ten or twelve, and I was also expected to make that extra money and bring it home to contribute to the family. Any opportunity a child had to contribute monetarily to the family fund was considered good fortune. If we rejected the opportunity, it might not be offered again. Others would be called first. Time for play would come some other day.

My brother Frank remembers having to go when he was twelve also, picking at first, then being moved to loading the boxes as they got filled. My grandmother's ultimate "encouragement" was to warn: "You don't want to be a *lanyusso!*" This meant "a lazy bum"; it was her worst insult and probably included everyone who did not work as hard or as continuously as she did. If I tried to defend myself by saying that the others were not working, she explained it with *"Sono lanyussi,"* meaning, "They are lazy!"

# *Work Ethic Admired*

Two situations from my father's working experience demonstrate his commitment to putting forth perfectionist effort. The first occurred when he worked at the Pittsburg Pioneer Rubber Mills (he was there for fifteen years before the incompetent supervisor incident related earlier). The other workers drafted Dad to be union president, partly based on his ideas for company improvement, which he had courageously taken to management and had explained so clearly and convincingly that the ideas had been implemented. The employees saw that management took Dad seriously.

Dad was no pushover, though. He believed the workers had to work smarter if they wanted more money. His philosophy simply was "If we want more money, the company has to get more money." So he insisted on cutting down on nonproductive periods. His work ethic was a great inspiration, and though they might not have been happy about losing their "down time," the other workers knew he was trustworthy and would speak for them unabashedly.

I learned about the second situation when I came home on furlough in 1944. (This was after Dad's decision to leave Pioneer, when Mom and I went to pick him up. He started working for Yuba; I went into the army. Fifteen months later, I was home on furlough, the same furlough that I had to demand, mentioned earlier). A buddy and I were in a store in Martinez when a woman recognized the name Bellecci. She asked if we knew Sal Bellecci. "Yes, he's my father."

"Oh, he's a marvelous person. Your father's going to win the war by himself!"

At home, I told Mom about the comment and asked what was going on. She informed me: "Oh, he's got all these women working for him at Yuba." Yuba Manufacturing was on the other side of the Carquinez Straits from Martinez, so anyone who worked at Yuba but lived in Martinez had to ride the ferry over. (The Martinez-Benicia Bridge has since been built.) Mom had met some of the women on those occasions when she drove down to the wharf to pick Dad up. Upon meeting Mom, the women would sing Dad's praises. This is why.

When Dad quit Pioneer and got the job at Yuba, he was put to work on the howitzers assembly line, which needed precise measurements to be made and reset throughout the day. A howitzer was a kind of short-barreled portable cannon used by the army and marines, and Yuba made the barrels. The women watched the machines and would shut the lathe off if it got off the precise measurement required, but then they had to wait for the next setting to be made.

The machinist whom Dad replaced had only been able to keep two or three lines working, whereas Dad kept ten lines moving. He did it by constantly walking up and down, making the precise adjustments on the lathes, chatting with the women while he worked and telling them, "When it gets to this point, call me." He was available when they called him (unlike his predecessor), as he did not believe in taking rest breaks or coffee breaks but worked steadily from start to lunch, and from after lunch to closing time. His predecessor had also belittled the women's efforts. Dad never did. Rather, his cooperative spirit improved the working environment for the women, raising their morale.

Such diligence and willingness to work hard was Dad's daily habit in life. He, just one person, made a huge impact in the company. That's why I was told: "He's going to win the war by himself." The Yuba Company was months behind in production of the howitzer artillery when he started, but he got them caught up and put them ahead of schedule. Recall that he made quite a bargain before going to work at Yuba. I think he was aware how his work ethic differed from others and knew that he would be more productive. He delivered beyond their wildest dreams. He remained at Yuba for twenty-five years until he was seventy, when he finally insisted on retiring, though they begged him to continue.

## The Power of Wise Teachers

Many people credit their teachers for various reasons. I believe the best teachers are those who know how to inspire a student to do his or her best and who teach that excellence takes more than first-draft papers or last-minute essays. Teachers can foster the habit of striving for excellence. I remember two teachers in particular who knew how to reach me.

My high school English teachers were determined that all the Alhambra High college prep students would pass the entrance English A Exam at UC Berkeley. This was no small feat as every applicant to the university (almost all were from California at that time) had to take the exam, and the passing rate was 50 percent. Our teachers wanted *every* Alhambra student to be in that passing group.

The exam task was to produce a three hundred-word essay in forty minutes with no errors in spelling, sentence structure, punctuation, or grammar. No notes were permitted. Our teachers prepared us for this task by challenging us to strive for excellence on each assignment.

They used different motivators for various students. Often one teacher, Ms. Wehe, less than five feet tall, graded my work A over F. The A was for content and the F for some mechanical error. That would equal a D+. Ms. Wehe would always look up at me, smile, and say, "John, you can do better, so I'll be a little stricter with you." I did not think that was fair. However, since I continued to strive for perfection, she obviously chose the right tactic for me.

(During a recent high school reunion, my classmates revealed that they had been jealous of me for being Ms. Wehe's favorite. I never felt like her pet, not with that A over F type of grading. But then I recalled that the next year, when my sister Marie was in her class, Ms. Wehe watched out for Marie also, often asking if she had had her milk that morning, since she looked a little pale. Maybe we were her favorites.)

The second teacher is remembered for her mercy when I made a mistake. During the second semester of my junior year in high school, I missed making the California Scholarship Federation (CSF) list by one point, having only two As and three Bs in the subjects that counted. My father considered education much more important than playing sports. He ruled that in the fall, which would be my senior year, I was not going to play football until I got back into the CSF. We had a new football coach who was counting on me to play, but with my father's dictate, I was sidelined. Mr. Knowles, the principal who had previously been the coach, saw me just watching during practice and asked what happened. I told him of my restriction. He realized I would miss the season, waiting for semester grades. Would I mind if he talked to my father? "Please do!"

Due to their talk, we negotiated that I would get a weekly report card, and as long as I had CSF grades (three As and one B were the minimum requirements), I could play. If I dropped below, I was through. Each Monday, I would get a grade from English, Latin, physics, trig, and world history. I played the whole season, though I had one very close call.

Ms. Hazel Murray, my Latin teacher, saved me. Fortunately, she had also been my teacher the previous year, when I took the New York state test for Latin in both first and second semesters, on which I made the highest scores recorded anywhere up to that time. Maybe that was the reason for her mercy when I made a B one week in Latin, missing an A by two points.

I was in major dismay when I saw that B. I went to Ms. Murray and explained the dire consequences of those two points. She graciously agreed to average that week's grade with the other weeks prior and gave me an A. I never dropped below an A in her class again. I would remember this demonstration of mercy as a means of encouragement when I became a supervisor. I believe she was willing to help me with this because of my excellent work earlier.

# Encourage the Use of Another's Capabilities

Excellence is needed in many aspects of our lives. It might be needed from us, but sometimes our task is to encourage it in those we know. My teachers knew how to bring it out in me. When I was in the military, I had a chance to help one of my buddies use his skills.

While I was in the South Pacific during the service, my company's task was to build a petroleum pipeline to serve the invasion force being developed for the Philippines, where Japan had a strong outpost. In mid-October of 1944, the Leyte invasion was under way. It was a joint amphibious effort by a very large Allied and American force, whose goal was to shut down the ports of Leyte Island to the Japanese and thus retake the Philippines from them. Planes were taking off from an aircraft carrier and an airport about ten miles from our dock unloading facilities. Three or four tankers were out in the bay, fully loaded with fuel for the planes, waiting to be unloaded.

My job as a private, first class (PFC) was pipeline patroller between our dock and the airport ten miles away. I came on duty as night descended and heard our crank-type phone ring. The voice on the other end said, "We need gasoline. Why aren't you pumping it?"

Just coming on duty, I answered, "I don't know."

"Well, we're invading Leyte. We need all the gas we can get." I walked the half-mile to the dock and saw the unloading facility lit up like it was Christmas, lights flooding the area, and officers from every branch of service standing and fuming. It seemed as if every tool known to humanity was spread out on the dock. The pump engines were in pieces on the dock around the pumps. I went to the captain and delivered the message from the airstrip.

"Can't you see? The pumps are all apart and won't work."

"Bob Brown can fix those engines," I said, giving him the name of a mechanically talented friend.

"Go get Bob Brown." He had no idea who Bob Brown was, since Bob was also a lowly PFC.

"Sir, he's up at main headquarters, and I don't have a jeep to get him."

"There's a jeep. Go get him." I drove up, found Bob, and told him they wanted him down at the dock, something to do with the engines for the pumps.

"What tools do I need?"

"Oh, I don't know ... pair of pliers, a screwdriver ..." I did not want to tell him any more for fear that he would refuse to go. We drove back to the dock. As we approached and Bob saw all the officers from the various armed services, he looked at me and called me a colorful name.

The captain directed him to get to work. Walking to the piles of parts, Bob kept calling me names, stunned at the job. I told him he could do it. I helped him, handing him tools. He had only one brief false start, then the pumps worked. All the brass from the various branches disappeared without a word as soon as the gas started flowing through the pipeline.

The captain told me that I had better go get my pipelines lined up to the airport; in other words, make sure everything was open for the gas, now able to be unloaded from the ships, to arrive at the airfield. I had long since checked and rechecked my responsibility, putting blinds (inserts used when pipes intersected) in the pipeline myself to direct the gasoline's journey to the airstrip with no possible errors. I told the captain, "Sir, this gasoline isn't stopping till it gets over Leyte."

"None of your wise remarks."

"Yes, sir."

The next day, thanks to his skills that literally saved our support of the military invasion, Bob Brown was suddenly made a staff sergeant, while two staff sergeants were demoted to private, not even private first class. (Apparently they were supposed to know how to fix the pump engines.) Within two months, the joint forces had achieved their war objective.

After the war, Bob Brown became vice president of research and development for a major automotive equipment manufacturer. His wife still likes to hear the story, every time we get together. It is an amazing example of the power of just one person willing to do his or her best, even with such a daunting task under very stressful circumstances.

## *Choosing a Life Partner*

When it came to marriage, it was expected that my siblings and I would marry within the Italian community, as the parents knew each other and assessed the children by the values of the parents. In a few cases, it appeared my mother was trying to set me up with the daughters of her friends, but these young ladies and I did not have much in common. I wanted someone who was college educated, who valued excellence as my family did, who could talk with me about serious matters, but who also could have fun with me.

Some people think they can change a person to have their values; I have rarely seen that turn out positively. I would advise dating only those people whose values match yours, especially the desire for excellence and willingness to work hard.

In 1948, I had been dating Ileane, taking her to ball games and movies. I learned about her great determination in completing nursing school, and

I could tell she appreciated excellence and doing a job right the first time. But she planned to go back to Montana, the place where her Norwegian immigrant grandparents had settled, to help her sister who was in the late stage of pregnancy. She did not know when she would come back to California. My mother told me that I needed to bring this girl I was dating home for dinner, so they could meet her. We worked it in before Ileane left for Montana.

When she first came to the family home for dinner, she met the immediate family, which included my maternal grandmother (whose house was across the backyard at that time), my parents, my two sisters, my brother and brother-in-law. I'm sure that was a little intimidating. Ileane was as naturally quiet as I was talkative, but she was, and still is, a very gracious person who can join in conversation easily.

We had dinner. After dinner, Ileane popped up from the table, went into the kitchen, and put on an apron to help my sisters with the dishes, without it even being mentioned. It really surprised my grandmother, who said in Sicilian dialect, "*Ci sono femini Americani che sono bono purro!*" meaning, "Some American girls are good too." I learned that Ma's concern was that I might decide to marry some girl who was a lazy housekeeper and would not take care of me properly. Ileane's initiative in helping with the dishes spoke well of her industrious nature. My grandmother, mother, father, sisters, and brother all approved. I waited for her to come back from Montana; then we married.

After we were married, Ileane worked as a nurse through her first pregnancy and then cared for our children and was an excellent homemaker, keeping the house very clean (antiseptic, actually) and managing the finances very thriftily as well. My grandmother really liked Ileane because she had extra education and status due to being a nurse. Ma saw Ileane as someone who was willing to work and take care of the children, as she had. Ileane did not learn Italian or Sicilian, but the two women somehow communicated.

A few years later, on the sad occasion when Marian DiMaggio, Dad's niece, got sick and was in the hospital, the family asked Ileane to be the nurse at the hospital even though she had young children at home. The relatives trusted her and wanted her. They took care of our children while Ileane went to take care of Marian at the hospital, to assist in providing round-the-clock care for the few weeks until Marian died. Years later, during Christmas visits to Martinez, while spending time downtown with my brother Frank and sister Marie, the relatives would see me and ask me how my wife was and tell me what a good woman she was and what a great help she had been for their sister.

It is important that your partner in life have values and a work ethic similar to yours. I chose a wonderful partner whose diligence and desire for excellence, love of family, and love of God dovetailed with mine. Perhaps it was Ileane's immigrant family background that gave us matching values and outlook on life. She was never afraid of hard work or long hours, doing whatever it took to make our family thrive. We did not differ on raising our children with high expectations and the value of working hard. She was also an extremely capable financial manager, comparing favorably with the best of the Sicilian women I knew. After almost sixty years, I treasure her companionship and values now more than ever.

## Caring Even When It's Not Your Job

It's one thing to expect the best of yourself and others when you are in charge or you have an active part. It's another thing to be a bystander and speak up when you see a problem forming. Some people might pass up a situation, thinking: *That's their problem,* or *No one's paying me to get involved.* Perhaps you might talk yourself out of intervening by thinking: *They are going to wonder who the heck I think I am.* Do not let those thoughts prevent you from speaking up to correct an error. Doing so can favorably affect you, and many others you do not even know, like ripples flowing outward from a rock dropped in water.

We moved from California to Illinois when I felt I had no room for advancement in the job at Dow Chemical. We stayed in Illinois for three years while I worked for Borden Chemical. For various reasons, we chose to move back to California. On my last day of work at Borden Chemical in April of 1964, after I had already turned in my resignation, I toured the plant. At the PVC plant floor, I smelled vinyl chloride, which is like propane as far as explosiveness is concerned. The operator on duty, a fellow by the name of Paul E., should have known (I am certain he did know) that if you smell it, it is very dangerous. He should have either aired out the floor or shut the plant down. I chewed him out since I was in the habit of correcting a person any time I witnessed a bad mistake like that in any plant I managed. Then I went on my way, without giving the incident another thought.

Twenty-five years later, after more professional moves among chemical companies, the same Borden Plant came under my jurisdiction again. I had a tour of the plant to see its present status. At each control room, I was asked if I had seen Paul. After the third of these, I was wondering why the whole plant was asking about this. It turned out that Paul, now in the maintenance shop, had told everyone he was sure that, when I saw him again, I was going to fire him. He thought I must surely remember the incredible operating safety error he had made. I did not remember it, but even if I had, I certainly would not have done any firing as soon as I arrived.

However, they told me that after Paul was corrected, no one at the plant had ever made *that* error again. The plant supervision and the workers never forgot it for another reason, too. Even though I had been severing ties with the company, I cared that it should be operating safely, so deep was my concern for all the people who were, and had been, my responsibility.

If you truly care for people, you will speak up when you are aware of an error that could cause harm to anyone if not corrected. It might be small, like ensuring someone cleans up a spill in a store, which saves another person from falling or breaking a bone, for example. It could be a larger issue, with the potential for life-or-death consequences. Whatever the circumstance, your responsibility to strive for excellence is important. And, like this situation, you never know when it will come back into play in your own life.

## Excellence Rewarded

The power of a reputation of excellence is never to be underestimated. When Dad was seventy-five years old, five years into retirement, PG&E called and asked him to come in and supervise the repair of their slide gate for a huge dam in the Sierra Nevada Mountains. He was amazed to have been asked. Of course, he did not want to go—he was retired! He told them he did not want to do the work. They said they just needed him to supervise; his reputation for attention to detail and willingness to correct to get something perfect made him the perfect candidate, even at the age of seventy-five.

When he discussed it with me on one of my visits to Martinez, I told him to ask for $1,000 a day, a consultant's fee. Dad thought I was crazy. I changed my mind and told him to ask for $2,000 per day. He said, "You big shots, you don't know what money is worth."

"Just tell them, Dad."

A month later I came back to visit again, and he reported incredulously, "They gave it to me, and they asked me how much more I wanted!"

Though he was surprised to find how much his excellence was valued, I was not. Having worked in several companies by then, I knew the impact of someone like Dad on achieving first-rate quality, good productivity, meeting deadlines, and high employee morale. His kind of work ethic is priceless and thus eagerly sought. People who want to succeed in this country would be wise to do the same, whatever their line of work.

# *Make It Permanent and Safe, Not Slipshod*

After my family moved to Louisiana, my brother and sisters and I invested in commercial property in the city of Baton Rouge. It has proven to be a worthwhile venture all these years. One situation provided the opportunity for a choice between high quality or quickly thrown together. Because of my habit and the experiences I have had where doing things right leads to success, you can probably guess which option I chose.

One particular facility has been rented for more than twenty-five years to a Toshiba copier supplier. We had expanded it once during those years, and this tenant again needed more warehouse storage space and asked me to build something that he had roughly drawn up. It looked like a lean-to shed. His primary focus was getting the job done quickly. He thought he would only need more storage for a short while anyway.

I told him I preferred to do it right so it would last a long time. My plan was to make it totally enclosed, on a concrete base, with electrical supply and an electrically operated overhead door. We did it the better way, as I wanted. It was initially a much higher cost to me, but its value raised the value of the site rather than make it look shabby. It has since been used much more than he expected, especially since hurricane Katrina, which wiped out New Orleans and made him the Toshiba supplier for the state of Louisiana. Just recently, Toshiba's American management came to tour the facility, and they were greatly pleased with it.

We had no idea of the future need of the expansion on this site. I just knew that it is better to build for permanence, rather than in haste. The best policy is to aim for excellence whenever possible.

Excellence does not just happen. It takes planning, attention to details, and consistent effort, sometimes a prolonged effort. That doesn't sound like much fun, does it? But as you have noted in these stories, these people had great personal satisfaction. My grandmother Ma knew her several jobs were helping provide not only for her family but for many others as well. The teachers were forming the future with their encouragement. My dad's commitment to excellence furthered the war effort, as did Bob Brown's. Those achievements are something that can never be taken away.

The toughest part of excellence is probably the willingness to stick with a job when it has unforeseen complications, when you're tired, when it's taking longer than it was supposed to, or when you just want to do something else. Those are the times when parents need to lovingly insist—as Mom did for her grocery needs, as Ma did on picking fruit, and as my dad did regarding good grades. Those are the times when a boss needs to respectfully correct, as Dad's co-workers and Paul E. were corrected. Those are the times you need people around you who have the values that will support intense effort, such as I provided for Bob Brown, and which Ileane has steadfastly provided for me all these years.

Don't be afraid of hard work. The rewards are your personal satisfaction, a good reputation that precedes you and follows you, and a safe and high-quality environment in which to live and work, and yes, even to play.

# Chapter Five: Hold No Grudges

People will purposely or accidentally cause problems and even traumas in our lives. Conflict and hurt come with living in the same home and sharing the same streets, stores, schools, and community services. It is often hard to emotionally let go of the visions of what might have been if the negative interaction not happened, thinking *"If only ..."* Also, we might find it very hard not to wish ill upon a person.

But doing either of those is not going to help a person on the road to success. Holding a grudge possesses people, so that they are no longer thinking clearly. Holding a grudge hurts the grudge-holder beyond the insult or loss that is already occurring, poisoning your heart and contaminating the present. To help yourself, release the hurts from your heart in order to keep living and enjoy the present moments.

Newcomers to an area or a country naturally have differences from most of the people already living there. Unfortunately, it was common for those who were different to be looked down upon and held in suspicion. The immigrants, indentured servants, and slaves of the past heard the words and could feel and see when they were unwanted or not liked. Today's immigrants will probably experience the same. They, and all who are hurting emotionally, have a choice. They can let those hurt feelings take control of their actions or let them go.

It is understandable that a person who is insulted or harmed, or loses something precious, will take offense. Acting unwisely in response, however, makes us end up in worse shape. Negative feelings can be channeled to correct injustice, as the energy from anger is used to change an unfair situation. When that is not possible, trying to understand the other's logic sometimes helps. But in any case, let go.

The following stories express a variety of experiences in which family members were able to find the wisdom to let go of resentment and thus continue on the road to success.

## *Third Grade Hurt*

During the third grade, a fellow student, non-Italian, became anemic and had to stay home for weeks to recover, taking cod liver oil three times a day. For at least six weeks, I went over to his house every afternoon to drop off and pick up his schoolwork, going inside and being offered a cookie and glass of milk. His father and my father had been friends when they were young. Both were machinists, though they did not work at the same plant.

The boy finally got well about the time of his birthday. I mentioned to my mother that he was having a birthday party, and she wanted to know what I wanted to get for him. I told her I was not invited. She immediately reacted with insult and got livid. "What? After all those weeks of you hauling his schoolwork for him, he doesn't invite you to his party?" She told me not to take his papers for him anymore.

Fortunately, I did not have to decide whether to obey her, since he was back in school. My mother took the non-invitation as a personal insult. The invitations went out through the PTA, to which his mother belonged, but my mother and the other two Italian mothers in my class did not. Certainly it would have been easy enough to hand me my invitation in class or at his home. I felt snubbed, but got over it.

Years later, between our junior and senior years in high school, that same boy bought an old Model A car, but did not really know how to fix it. Since I did, I offered to help. The car was brought to our house and put in our garage for the two weeks it took for me to get it running. My parents were willing to allow this; my mother was not carrying a grudge. The car owner's contribution was to go and buy the parts. When the car was running, he offered to pick me up each morning for school, and he did so consistently, showing up at 8:00 a.m. and waiting patiently for me for a few minutes since I always seemed to be running late.

I picked up the habit of being helpful from observing my father, who offered help to others whenever he could. Holding no grudge from years before enabled me to be open to an opportunity to do something good. In this case, the goodwill that flowed outward in my offer to fix the model A resulted in my receiving a ride to school each day. I didn't expect the ride or offer my help in order to get it, but I was glad to receive it.

# World War II Living Restrictions

With the Japanese attack on Pearl Harbor in December of 1941, the issue of security in the United States was critical. It is common knowledge that the Japanese were herded into camps, but less well known is that Italians were also under suspicion.

The Italians who were noncitizens were ordered to move at least eight miles from any coastline because of possible submarine sightings along the California coast. This was to prevent any traitors or spies from signaling to an oceangoing vessel. However, in our area, all the Italians who were ordered to move were from sixty to eighty years old, and ironically, they had children in the armed services.

My uncle Frank was in the army, yet his mother (my grandmother Ma) was moved; another relative forced to move had two sons in the armed services. My grandparents on both sides, and their friends, were considered "threats" and were uprooted from their homes in Martinez, Crockett, and Pittsburg to be relocated in the suburbs of Concord. My parents quickly found and rented an old home, a shack almost, for them in Concord.

Meanwhile, since most of them could speak little or no English, I was instructed to write letters to present their case. (Being a university student, I was expected to know everything, including how to present their case and to whom.) This is often the situation with children of immigrants: as the one who interprets for the family, he or she is expected to be able to navigate through many agencies and know how to accomplish any interaction with the new society.

So I did write the letters, addressing them to the Commandant located in San Jose. I expressed our conviction that it was nonsense that these people were being forced to move when their own children and grandchildren were fighting for the United States. Additionally, my father and other adult children of those forced to move were taking their turns to volunteer at night as spotters for enemy aircraft. Many members of the family were supporting the country as best they could.

After several letters, we received word that the "aged and the infirm" would be permitted to return to their homes. My relatives had thought it was unfair that they had been moved out, but they never bad-mouthed the government. They could understand the reason for the move, in theory, believing the United States was justified in making such a move, since they were at war with Italy, Japan, and Germany. They chose to let go of the insult and to hold a positive spirit until the end of their lives. They were very happy with the successes they had achieved because of relocating in their adopted country. It did not spoil those successes when the government acted bureaucratically.

Whether foreigners are moved to another land by force or live there voluntarily, they are especially vulnerable during a war between their native country and their host (or new) country. In this present time, as the United States struggles with armed conflicts and war in the Mideastern and other regions, people often tend to be suspicious of those with Arab or Moslem heritage, even those who might have been in this country for many years. The wise response of the "foreign" person is to go about one's daily work, always acting with the values presented in this book, and offering some volunteer service to the country or community as well. That will help build the goodwill of the people in the host country.

## *Easy Come, Easy Go*

Injustice can occur not only between ethnic groups, but within families as well. As noted in the introduction, my dad's brother Frank was twenty years older than my dad. Frank was a good brother to Dad in his growing-up years, and Dad never forgot the loyalty he owed "Tzuchico". (Chico is short for Francisco; "Tzu" is a sign of respect, meaning "Mister".) I'm sure it must have been a hard blow when Tzuchico's children, after his death, cheated my dad. But Dad chose to forgive and let it go, and he did it for us. Here is the story.

When some years passed and my dad saw that his brother depended on his own children for his livelihood, Dad wanted to help Tzuchico become financially independent. His plan was to use some property in downtown Martinez that had been purchased by their parents, which Dad had inherited, build commercially, and then share the rents with Tzuchico. (The reason Dad alone inherited that particular property was because it was purchased with the earnings that Dad, as a sixteen year-old, had received from work and turned over to *his* mother, according to the custom. Those earnings accrued for nine years, the time Dad worked prior to getting married.)

To clear that downtown Martinez property, Dad had one house torn down while the other, in which we three older children were born, was moved out to Concord, where we modernized it for my sister Marie's first house. (That is the house we were working on when my brother Frank left and walked eight miles home.) Once the land in downtown Martinez was cleared, Dad had a commercial building put on it. He paid for the building outright, then signed over one-quarter to his brother Tzuchico, and one-quarter to his sister Marian Aiello as well, retaining half-ownership for himself. (Though Marian owned and collected rent from four residential properties already, Dad wanted to be fair and did not want Tzuchico to feel like he was getting a handout.) His brother thus gained some financial independence from his own children and lived out the rest of his days in a more contented manner.

Tzuchico's will stipulated that Dad be given the opportunity to *buy* back the one-quarter that he had given to his brother for the price it was when given. However, Dad did not know this was in the will, and my cousins did not tell him, nor did their lawyer. Dad continued the upkeep on the property and, some months after his brother died, went to the cousins who inherited it and requested their share of the payment for upkeep. They refused, saying they did not want to put any more money in it, and made a reference such as, "You did not buy us out when you had the chance, so why are you bothering us with this now?" Dad did not know what they were talking about. When shown the will, he was very surprised. He expressed his desire to buy the one-quarter share. My cousins were divided as to how that should occur. One wanted it given back at no charge, since their dad had been given it for free. Another thought the lower price was fair, but the others wanted the market price then, commenting that "Salvaturino" (Dad's nickname) had the money. Eventually Dad paid the larger amount and reclaimed the share.

My sisters and brother and I were aghast. "Dad! What are you doing? Letting these people cheat you?" We wanted him to negotiate, to bargain down the price.

He told us his thinking: "When I'm gone, you will inherit this. I don't want you to have any conflicts with the family. Let's just get it done with and not cause any upsets with the family." We swallowed hard, but it was not easy to let go of our strong feelings of disagreement.

Then we heard that with part of the money, one of our cousins bought his son a brand-new, very fancy car, and we shook our heads at the extravagant use of money for which our dad had worked so hard. Within a few weeks, that son had smashed his brand-new car. My brother Frank, upon hearing the story from our cousin, told him, "Well, easy come, easy go!" Though we never wished anyone ill, we felt that some justice had occurred. But as Dad had predicted, there was no friction about that building anymore, and we were able to remain friends with our cousins, twenty years older than us, until they passed away.

## *Doctors Are Not Perfect*

My younger brother Anthony was a typical toddler, playing and climbing and not remembering all the instructions to be careful. One wash day, when he was two years old, he fell in the pot of hot laundry water and got burned on a large part of his body, particularly his back. My mother was frantic and took him to the hospital for treatment. The doctor saw that his wounds were cleaned and left instructions for his care, and then went duck hunting.

All could have been okay, but little Tony started to have complications. The nursing staff could not locate the doctor, out on his hunt. The other doctors in town refused to take over the case, not wanting to be responsible for another doctor's patient and a plan of treatment that they did not start. Tony did not receive the needed care, and he died.

I was a child, only about seven or eight years old, but I remember my mother getting angry, really angry; I never saw her that angry before. It was understandable, of course, but I did not understand what had occurred. My mother told the doctor, "I'm never coming back to you again!" and something like, "I hope you get treated the way you treat others." But *her* mother, Ma, encouraged her to think of her other children who might need care; she pointed out that he'd been a good doctor before, and so forth. Though I did not know it then, Ma had also lost a child to an accident; her son died because of firecrackers. Ma's wisdom was born out of coping and continuing in spite of her grief.

Some time later, my younger sister Marie had severe stomach cramps. The different doctor in town was not very good and misdiagnosed the trouble, giving my sister the wrong kind of care, and she only got worse. At my grandmother's urging, my mother decided to take Marie to the doctor who had neglected Tony. Marie had gotten so ill by this time that the doctor said she had to be put in the hospital and have surgery, or he would not take the case. She had a ruptured appendix, and he thought she might not make it even with surgery.

My mother agreed to the hospitalization. Marie had to stay in the hospital for two weeks while the wound drained, as they did not have the antibiotics that are available now. My mother stayed with Marie during the critical time, making sure the nurses did what they were supposed to and that they were going to call the doctor for any unusual situation (or she would have called him herself). In this situation, holding a grudge might have cost my mother a second child's life.

## *Regular Squabbles*

There were always some arguments in the fishing community about who was first and second, but no grudges were held. I did not realize this at first. It seemed to me as a young child a very contentious thing. These men were at each other's throats, then suddenly it was over, and they would go drink with each other that evening or the next day. *"Si, si, e bono,"* meaning, "Yes, yes, it's okay," they would say after considerable argument. I finally realized that this was how the men discussed problem areas among themselves.

Their ability to get over any disagreements without holding a grudge was important, for an immigrant group, or any group in the minority, needs its members to provide emotional and physical support to each other. Fractures that persist in these communities will weaken the newcomers' ability to settle in and succeed, or the minority group's ability to advance.

## *See What You Do Have*

The trauma of coping with the loss of a child occurred in our generation as well. Ileane, my wife, was close to delivery of our third child when we lived in Concord, California, in 1953. She took the bus to the doctor's office in Berkeley and, after the exam, felt something was not quite right as she waited to take the bus home. It was a Friday. She did not feel like things were right the whole weekend and went to the doctor again on Monday. The child had died. (We later learned it was due to placenta previa, in which the placenta has attached in the womb in a vulnerable location—near the opening of the birth canal—becoming detached as labor begins, causing the unborn child to suddenly lose his or her lifeline. Scientists estimate that it occurs in one of five hundred births.)

Ileane had to go through labor anyway and had severe bleeding. The nurses were reluctant to call the doctor till the last second; they did not want to bother the doctor in the middle of the night. I was really concerned. We had lost the baby, and now I almost lost Ileane. She needed several transfusions totaling five pints of blood, and she was in the hospital for a week. I went back and forth from the hospital to my folks' house, wanting to be with my wife, while trying to help out with our two children whom my mother was keeping. I managed to keep going in the midst of the grief because of the need to focus on these two kids that we did have, who were staying at their grandmother's, crying and crying. It was rough on everyone.

My mother always remembered the scene when Ileane finally did come back from the hospital. Our daughter Karen was on the swing outside with my mother. Karen got up and ran to see if it were really her mother, then stopped about halfway when she could see that it was, made a big smile, and turned around to skip happily back to the swing. My mother was mystified: "Darn kid, she's been crying and crying for days, and now she doesn't even hug her mother!"

Ileane was more forgiving of the doctor and the whole situation than I was; she knew holding a grudge only tears you up inside, and she picked up at home where she had left off, though obviously terribly saddened. Two years later when our fourth child Linda was born, Ileane went to the same doctor. Others were available; yet she believed he had done his best in the situation.

It took me more time to forgive. I eventually realized that you have to pick up the life that you have, caring for the children you do have. I could tell I was past holding a grudge when I could discuss our loss without strong feelings arising.

Often a person's first reaction to betrayal or loss is anger. It is understandable. However, psychologists tell us that anger is a secondary emotion, fueled by hurt or disappointment. In order to let go of many situations of grief, including those presented above, we had to let go of the feeling of anger, which is like a protection from the hurt or disappointment. Sooner or later, we came to terms with the sadness, often with tears shed in private. When we did allow the sadness to be expressed, those strong feelings could pass through us and not harm the rest of our decision-making and relationships. The freedom this brings is an important element in anyone's happiness and, ultimately, in their success.

# Chapter Six: Take Advantage of Educational Opportunities

Many people come to America because it is known as the "Land of Opportunity." Once they arrive, it is natural to seek out others of their background for comfort amid the unfamiliar. However, to find the opportunities, start learning. A person who wants to learn is usually welcomed in any culture. While we did notice cliques in my hometown school, neighborhood, and workplace, as well as among those who refused to allow newcomers to join socially, we encountered many more people who appreciated a hard worker and an enthusiastic learner, no matter what the other's culture or background. Such people understood that this country needs the best in whatever skills and talents everyone can give, regardless of their ethnic or racial heritage.

Education is an important doorway to discovering, expanding, and refining those skills and talents. This chapter highlights situations that demonstrate the importance of getting an education, or going back and continuing your education, as a way to achieve your goals. It was a new experience, this universal access to education, as that was not the situation in Italy or Sicily. First some background on that.

## The Difference in Availability of Education

In Italy, everyone started school at eight years old and had four years of basic education. Only the presumed smart or the wealthy students went on to high school and got a full education. In Sicily, high school was only open to the landowners' children. My grandmother, Ma, as energetic and motivated as she was, only went to the fourth grade, telling us that only the very smart ones went another two years, and that was all year round. However, other relatives thought that money, not intelligence, was really the factor. Those money-privileged students were able to attend two more years if they wished; then, by the time they were sixteen, they were eligible for college.

At my high school graduation, I was reminded by one of the relatives that I was lucky to be in America, where anyone could go to college, even if you were not rich. My family was obviously not wealthy; my father was a machinist, working for a daily wage, and my mother, like most women of her time who were married and had children, worked only at home. I was planning to go to college and would be the first one in the Italian fishing community from our town to do so.

## Expressing the Family's Expectations

Grandfather John developed high expectations for me, even though I was not his first grandchild, typically the one on whom such pressure is put. The difference was that shortly after my birth, he perceived I was looking at him with intelligence and curiosity, so it was determined that I would be an engineer. At six months of age, either my parents or grandparents bought me a two-inch-thick volume of very thin onionskin paper pages, entitled *The Standard Dictionary of Facts.* As early as I could remember, that was it: I was going to be an engineer. My duty and career were chosen for me. As I look back now, perhaps I would have liked the field of law, but engineering was a good fit also, with many problems to solve and opportunities to contribute to society.

Grandfather John would hold me and point out the single light cord and bulb hanging in the center of the ceiling of some of the rooms in his house. He told me that we knew it was not magic that made the light work; it was something in the wires. When I grew up, I was going to know all about what went on in those wires. I must do well at school, so that when it came time to learn important, complicated things, I would be selected for the highest school available. He was drawing on his experience that in Italy, only the very brightest or wealthiest sons went on to high school and then to college ("*colegio*"). However, in the early 1900s, it probably was not much different in the United States.

# Get Vocational Training

When my father completed school in 1914, my grandfather said he needed to know something besides "just school". Dad had applied for a job at Mare Island Naval Base (the biggest base on the West Coast till after WW II), but there was no work for one with no training. So, practicality overcoming anxiety, Dad went on the train each day to Oakland and attended school all day at Polytechnical College, learning the skills needed for machine shop work in which measurements were down to the thousandth of an inch. Then this quiet sixteen year-old would ride the train back each night, day after day, for six months. Sometimes if there were no seats available, the conductors would let him ride free. When he finished the schooling, he again applied at Mare Island and this time was hired with enthusiasm because of his training. Immediately he earned the reputation of being a fast and accurate machinist. When World War One began, he continued to work at the machine shop in the naval base.

Today the situation is similar. Education through high school is necessary for good communication and math skills to navigate in our society; it is necessary to know the world's history, and to know enough about science to understand many aspects of life and nature. But even after a very good high school education, today's employers want workers with some extra knowledge, specific to what their business's needs are. Getting vocational training or a college degree is a very marketable plan and will head a person in the direction of success.

# Being Bilingual at School

Immigrants deal with the issue of communication with their new country. Their children are often more flexible linguistically. Since I spent as much time with both sets of grandparents as I did at home, I grew up to five years old not really knowing that English and Italian (or Sicilian, the dialect we spoke) were separate languages. None of my grandparents ever learned to speak English, though my maternal grandmother could read and write Italian. My conversations with all the grandparents were always in the Sicilian dialect. But my parents, aunts, and uncles spoke in English to me, using Sicilian in some circumstances. The kids in the neighborhood that I played with talked like I did, a mixture of English and Sicilian dialect, using whichever words expressed the idea more easily.

My kindergarten teacher, Ms. Townsend, enjoyed the way I would mix both languages though I, of course, did not realize I was doing so. When she had a substitute, I answered a question as I usually did. The substitute, Ms. Stone, whacked me on the head and stored me in the coat closet. I did not know what I had done wrong, but after the second time with Ms. Stone I was not going back to that school. Did I tell my mother I would not go? No! I was smarter than that, even at five years old. I took my snack bag, left the house at the regular time, and went to my maternal grandmother's house, since she lived only seven or eight blocks away. I told Ma there was no school and that I would rather spend the day at her house and in that area. My mother did not suspect anything, because I left the house and came home at the regular time, changed clothes, and went out to play.

At first Ma thought kindergarten must be different because her children still living at home (my mother as the oldest was only twenty-three at that time) had to go to school. But after three or four days of this, she became suspicious. Ma asked my mother why I did not have to go to school. Obviously, that blew the whole deal. The next day I was pretty well dragged all the way to school. Thank goodness Ms. Stone never again appeared, and I knew I must never have attendance problems anymore.

## Helping a Child Value School

When Grandfather John heard that I went to citizenship class with my father one night when I was twelve, and that I was the only one who knew the answer to the questions (and I was a child among all adults learning the social studies lessons for citizenship), he was extremely proud. Since children often don't see the reason to work hard for a goal that is years away, he showed his pride in a wise way. Grandfather John gave me five dollars as partial payment to get a bicycle: "See, if you do well in school, you'll be better off," he said. Bicycles cost about twelve or thirteen dollars, and only the well-to-do could give them to their children. He gave me a very special gift, and I used it to buy a used bike for about eight dollars.

My wife Ileane and I wanted to help our grandchildren see the same profit in education. We did not offer a bicycle, though, because that did not have the same impact today. We offered a cash reward to each of our seven grandchildren, to be given after they graduate from college. So far, three graduates have collected, two others are in college, and the youngest two are finishing high school and plan to go to college.

I still consider it an honor that people in this country are able to attend college. I know it gives a person an advantage over most of the people in the whole world, not just in our country.

## *Advocating When You See the Potential*

My grandfather John never did speak English; I do not know how literate he was - probably not very much. Yet, he saw in me one grandchild who should not be deterred from a full education. Though he died when I was thirteen, by that time he had communicated his belief in my potential to my maternal grandmother Ma, who was his niece, and who had a high respect for her uncle. She carried on the support for my continuing education. Ma was a natural one to encourage since, when she worked at the cannery, she noticed who got to be the boss and how those with education got ahead. She realized the need for leadership abilities and problem-solving skills in a supervisor. Among the relatives and the Italian community, Ma repeatedly defended my choice for continuing my education, since they still considered it a better practice for the sons to begin earning money for the family coffers as soon as possible.

## *When A Child Needs Encouragement*

My fourth-grade teacher, Ms. Elsie Cox, saw that when I was through with my morning's written work, I would squirm and fidget and disturb the nearby students. She permitted me to go out to morning recess early, to "save the diamond." The rule at school was that the first person standing on home plate at the beginning of recess got to have his class play on that particular baseball diamond. The class, the teacher, and I were all happy with that solution, and I did my work. Ms. Elsie also read an adventure story or a geographical story each day, which enthralled me; she held weekly spelling bees, and I looked forward to those competitions.

Ms. Watson, the librarian, was another person who bent the rules to encourage and support me. Three books a week was the limit anyone in sixth grade or below could check out at a time, but in the summer between fourth and fifth grades, I was reading my three and my cousin Nino's three books each week. Ms. Watson told me I should not check out so many books unless I was going to read them. She thought three was a large number per week. I told her that during the summer I read not three each week but six: mine and Nino's. She did not believe me and decided to quiz me on each of the books we had just brought in. When she realized that I had indeed read them all, she removed any restrictions on the number of books I could check out and even began recommending books that I might find interesting.

Both women were willing to make an adjustment that helped me love school and love learning, rather than be bored or be labeled a behavior problem. Many teachers today are willing to do the same for children who want to learn: encouraging a particular interest that will keep them connected with school. If you are a parent, relative, or neighbor, or know of such a child, talk to the teacher, with an interpreter if necessary, and advocate for the child.

## *Don't Let Poor Leadership Stop You*

One of the ways my brother Frank connected to school was through athletics. Yet this connection was disrupted due to prejudice against Italians. Frank persevered and continued with school and sports, which had a positive outcome.

When Frank was a junior in high school, a new physical education teacher / athletic director was hired who had been a track star at the University of California. Frank joked that this man, Mr. V, was so fast, he could run backwards faster than Frank could run forwards. But that was the end of the camaraderie. Though he knew the sport of track, he did not know about football strategy, nor did he have baseball expertise.

And for some reason, Mr. V did not like Italians. Frank noticed that the football practice scrimmage squads had the Italians on one team and everyone else on the other, but the Italians constantly won, having bigger players. In the other sports seasons, most of the Italians played baseball, while those with non-Italian backgrounds ran track. Once, when the Italian athletes challenged the track team to a meet and beat them, Mr. V was really annoyed with the Italians.

For the next-to-last grading period, Mr. V arbitrarily gave Frank an F in P.E. It so happened that the principal of the school, Mr. Knowles, lived up the hill from the family, and he would often give Frank a ride if it rained or if Frank was running late. When Knowles asked how things were going on one such ride, Frank told him of the grade of F. "Why, I can't do anything about that!" Knowles told him, but he did say he would see what he might find out. Soon, Frank's F was changed to a D, which was considered a passing grade. Mr. V lasted only that single year in our high school.

The next year new coaches were hired, men named Boschetti and Drexel. Frank, now a senior, did his best, as usual, and these new coaches saw Frank's potential and leadership ability. Frank was MVP in football, playing center for the team, and was captain of the baseball team (on which he had been varsity catcher for three years). He saw much more playing time under the new coaches. His level of respect for them was very high, since he realized that they knew the sports they were coaching. I am sure they thought well of him also. To his credit, Frank always played the sports he wanted to play, in spite of the poor leadership shown by the former track star hired to coach. He did his best, regardless.

And what were the expectations for Frank's grades? Frank recalls that during the time I was in the army, our mother and father were worried sick about me and did not even ask him about grades for the three years I was gone. (What a difference from my constant inspections, as noted earlier.) When the war was over, my mother looked at Frank's report cards and exclaimed happily to him, "Look at all these As and Bs you made!" I assume he appreciated their pride in him, even though it was delayed.

## Defending the Value of Education

The Italian community in Martinez and surrounding areas was like many human communities, comparing accomplishments of the offspring and feeling due pride. At the same time, there could be a note of ridicule from friends and relatives in the Italian community when someone's child did not meet expectations. After I graduated from high school, my mother endured much gloating from her peers because their sons went straight to work, making money to buy their families new sofas or the like, while I was still going to college and only spending money, not earning any. I was not helping the family out economically, which was seen as the most important duty, especially of the oldest son. As noted previously, my grandmother Ma supported extended education and helped my mother withstand the ridicule that her smart son was not making any money. Ma would tell the others, "Your grandson works at Shell; my grandson is going to be a boss" (a superintendent).

The fishermen did not give my father a hard time, however. They thought very well of my father and believed that if he had gone to high school, to say nothing of college, he could have been "a boss." They knew that getting more education was valuable, especially since during various fishing outings, my education had proven helpful.

In the tenth grade, I had carved a salmon out of wood and wrote an illustrated report on its life cycle, winning a first prize at the California State Fair. Thanks to learning that information, I had told the fishermen about the life cycle of the salmon, answering their questions of how salmon made their young and how many times they came back and forth down the river.

As it turns out in minority communities, at my college graduation, the relatives who had previously gloated about their sons now bragged about me, "You're going to be a boss. One of ours will be a boss." My personal goals were to be much more than a "boss" or supervisor, but this was the highest level with which they were familiar, and they were jubilant.

I eventually became a group vice president in charge of four plants in three states, which was certainly higher than a "boss." But I have seen how various ethnic groups take pride whenever someone from their group achieves such a worthy goal. One person's accomplishment somehow lifts up all in that group, as if showing the world what someone like them can do. Such pride honors the one who achieves. I was glad to be thought well of, after all the work I had done in college. The next section is about how I went about getting that education; that is, taking steps to get the courses I thought I would need in the future.

## *Changing the Curriculum at Berkeley*

Colleges and universities have set the courses they think a student will need in a particular field of study, and this usually works well for the students. This story is about the need to push for the variety of courses I wanted and thought I would need.

In the fall of 1946, after the war, I was back at the University of California, Berkeley. I was still in the college of chemistry, with an engineering major. Required courses for the College of Chemistry's engineering major included math, sciences, engineering, chemistry, and chemical engineering. I wanted to add in some letters and science classes, such as commercial law, human genetics, geology, accounting, production organization, management, and so on. We had to have an advisor sign for our courses. My advisor would not hear of it. I was already late in enrolling, due to working in the salmon fishing boats, so I boldly said, "I want to see the dean."

"Dean Latimer?" came the surprised reply.

"Yes."

"Okay, your funeral."

Two days later I went to see Dean Latimer, Nobel Prize winner, dean of the College of Chemistry. I was nervous but determined, especially since I had a new perspective on what I was good at and what I wanted to do, thanks to serving in the military. I explained to the dean that I wanted to take classes outside of chemistry and engineering because I could not see myself as a researcher or a lab analyst. He quickly agreed to my plan and the choices but stipulated that I had to maintain the proper grade point average in all courses to stay in the College of Chemistry; otherwise, the degree would be a Bachelor of Arts from the College of Letters and Science instead of a

Bachelor of Science from the College of Chemistry. I thanked him profusely, determined not to disappoint him or myself.

I knew I could do the work required in these extra classes. My GPA remained satisfactory, and my degree is a BS from the College of Chemistry. Surprisingly, this plan that I laid out became the normal curriculum for future chemical engineers. I heard about this when I arrived home one weekend late in the semester and found both of my parents sitting at the table with glum and disturbed looks on their faces. I asked what happened; they said, "The dean called. He wants you to call him back. Why is the dean calling?" I told them I had not failed; I was in no trouble, and I did not know why the dean was calling. Of course, I called Dean Latimer immediately and learned that it was a congratulatory call. It turned out that the College of Chemistry had been considering a curriculum change to include courses similar to what I had undertaken, and he had agreed to my changes partly to use me as a test case.

The new plan proved to be a well-rounded curriculum that prepared engineers for the various demands in management. Many times in my career I have used the information and insights gained from the extra courses I took those two years at college. Education is never wasted, and those years in particular formed me for the beginnings of management. I am proud that my diploma has the signatures of Earl Warren, Governor; Robert Sproul, University President; and Wendell L. Latimer, Dean of the College of Chemistry. All were men of distinction in their fields.

## *Moving Up Does Take Time*

Education opens up such exciting new worlds and concepts to graduates that they often feel ready to take on the world. However, applying all that book knowledge to everyday working situations takes time. Gaining experience is extremely important, and every graduate needs to be aware that connecting the appropriate book knowledge to each situation is the key. This does not diminish the importance of education. Education will give one a chance at employment, and a new kind of learning starts at that point.

When I had a job interview with Shell just prior to graduation, my father was so convinced of the power of education that he expected I would be able to tell the Shell Corporation that I would only work at the Martinez refinery! Shell offered me a job in Houston or Los Angeles (at the top pay rate at that time: $298 per month), but my father was not happy with that. He insisted that I tell them to place me at Martinez. I had no such power in those early years. It would be much later before I would have such leverage with any company. At that time, agreeing to move to Houston or Los Angeles was out of the question. The Italian family expectation was that I would remain close to home, and I was not willing to go against that at this point.

However, my father did take pride in my business accomplishments. Once I was visiting in Martinez in tandem with a business trip in San Francisco to negotiate with plant managers, vice presidents of Shell Chemical and other major chemical companies, all multibillion-dollar corporations. I was dealing with people on a much higher level than supervisors, and once my father realized it, he made sure all the relatives knew of the level of management I had reached. In fact, at the end, he was slightly disappointed that I was not president of all of Borden (I was "only" president of a Borden Chemical Division and a group vice president of the corporation). I had to make many moves with my family, though sometimes I refused to move my family. I had to leave jobs that were good but offered no advancement. Moving up did take time, but my education prepared me well.

## Get the Needed Education and Use it Wisely

When I came to Borden in Geismar, the lab supervisor was Sam B., a black man who had a college degree in business administration, not in the sciences. He was ineffective in his position, but had been put there as a kind of "tokenism." He knew he was not well suited to the job. I soon moved him to the purchasing department, which was at the same pay scale. He excelled in that position and remained there for over twenty-five years, continuing after I retired.

It so happened that working in the lab was another black man who did have a college degree in chemistry, John K. He knew the details of the lab processes and had the ability to organize and follow through, and he decided to apply for lab supervisor. Thanks to his education and work ethic, he received the job. Under his supervision were five white men and one black woman, Johnny Faye. Her road to the Lab involved personal initiative and the trust that we would honor our system.

Johnny Faye had a clerk's job in the office of the plant. She wanted to work in the lab, which would earn a higher salary, but she had no chemistry. We told her we would not even consider her without it. She knew we were not promising her anything, but she also saw that she was not going to get what she wanted without more education. Over the course of a couple of years, she took the three chemistry courses we required, passed them all, and then applied for the lab. When the next opening in the lab came up, she was considered like all the other applicants, and she did have all the qualities we needed for the position. We hired her. She proved to be an excellent addition to the lab. She enjoyed her new duties and the higher pay that went along with them. But had she not gone back to school but only sat and felt sorry for herself or complained that "we" weren't giving her a chance, she would not have had such an opportunity.

## *The Outcome*

I was the first Italian descendant from those early immigrants in Martinez to graduate from a regular four-year university or college. UC Berkeley had the reputation of being one of the finest colleges of the day, and I studied extremely long hours. We had as big a party for my college graduation as Ileane and I did for our wedding a year later.

Family expectations did not diminish for the next generation: both my brother's oldest daughter and our oldest daughter became doctors. All of my parents' thirteen grandchildren attended college, as mentioned in the opening chapter.

In today's world, many industries will not even grant an interview to someone who does not have a college diploma. But also in today's world, any student can get into college. Every state has a community college system, and the federal government gives grants and loans. Young men and women might be eager to make some money after high school, but parents would do well to encourage them to go to college; even attending part-time at a community college would be a tremendous benefit to get them started in higher education. They can do that while still holding a job during the day.

Additionally, many companies offer to reimburse tuition for employees who want to further their education and keep a high GPA. Some offer training opportunities on site. If a person is willing to put in the extra effort, job advancement through education is available. For those who want to succeed in this country, vocational training or higher education is a necessity.

# Chapter Seven: Have Faith, and Trust God

What is important about faith, and why would an immigrant, or anyone, for that matter, be better off having it? And what does it have to do with achieving success? This chapter will address those issues.

Faith is more than believing there is a God; it is believing that God is on your side. Immigrants often feel quite alone amid the foreign words, music, signs, and dress of another culture. Faith confirms that you are never alone. Our faith is based on the Christian Scriptures and the Roman Catholic Tradition, which tell us that Jesus is the Son of God who has revealed most fully what God was like. "He went around doing good and healing all those oppressed by the devil, for God was with Him" (Acts 10:38 NAB). He directed people to God and laid down His life on the cross for the truth of His message. Then His followers saw Him after He rose from the dead, and their belief formed the Church.

When we exercise our faith, it means we refuse to be held by the oppression of the devil, refuse whatever physical or emotional temptation, and turn to God instead. It means we believe that God has a big picture, and the message of the cross is that what seems terrible right now can come to some good. We are never abandoned; God always loves us. A faith-filled person holds on to that, even when things go wrong. Our best attitude is gratitude, to surround ourselves with the awareness of the blessings we have received.

# The Religious Practices and Faith of the Old Country

The religious practices and beliefs of Grandfather John and his generation were from the old country. Theirs was a faith that connected with God through regular religious practices, which is not to say their faith was routine. It was fostered through regular attention, such as eating fish, not meat, each Friday. They celebrated the holidays and feast days by going to Mass, their common worship, but most of the men did not go to Mass every Sunday for two reasons: though most of the prayers were in Latin, the homily was now in English, which they did not understand. Additionally, they had work to do related to the upkeep of the boats and repair of the nets. Once when an Italian-speaking priest offered a mission (preaching and prayer on a three or four weeknights in a row, for the purpose of refreshing the people's faith), the church was filled up each weeknight. One can assume that had parts of the Sunday worship service been offered in their own language, the Italian community would have found it a great source of encouragement.

Yet faith is more than what a person expresses through his or her religious practices. Faith includes the steadfast inner trust one places, day in, day out, in a Power greater and wiser than oneself. People in our family had a strong faith, evident in the following stories.

# Surviving the Spanish Flu

When my father was nineteen or twenty, he contracted the Spanish flu, as did many of the young adults around the world who did not have the immunity acquired by their elders in a similar flu pandemic some forty or fifty years before. This was a terrible time, because the flu hit many members of the young generation who had survived the Great War (World War I).

My father and a cousin were very sick, and unfortunately, the cousin did die. A doctor came to visit my father, who was being cared for by Marianna Russo, not then his mother-in-law. (Dad's own mother was not healthy at this time; Marianna, his first cousin who was fourteen years older than he, became his mother-in-law about six years later.) The doctor held out no hope for dad at all, expecting the flu would kill him also. Yet my father refused to die. Marianna attended Mass daily, praying particularly for him, and she declared that he was not going to die. They both had an iron will. Somehow, with prayer and steadfast care, my father did survive that flu.

About a year later, my father had reason to go to the doctor again. The doctor expressed sorrow about his cousin Sal Bellecci, who had died. My dad told him he had no cousin Sal Bellecci. "Yes," the doctor said, "the one who died of the flu."

Dad exclaimed, "That was me! I'm Salvador Bellecci! And I did not die!" The doctor was completely amazed.

## *Have Faith during Loneliness*

That same Marianna Russo, Ma, went to Mass every day in spite of not knowing English. She would consider it time to pray, which is to open oneself to God's point of view, get a holy and new perspective on things, and be refreshed for the day to come. On Sundays she looked forward to the hearing the music, which uplifted her spirit, and she would go to whichever Mass had it. But during all her years of excellent work and steadfast family support, she had an inner longing to visit her own family in Sicily. Though she proved to be adventurous in her many activities, it seems she was taken by surprise with how much she missed her immediate family. She wanted reassurance of their love for her. Her story of faith involves constancy during her years of loneliness.

After she married in Sicily in 1900, Marianna and her husband Tony Russo moved almost immediately to Black Diamond, California, now Pittsburg. Her husband's whole family came, including the father, Joseph Russo, and his four children along with their spouses. Perhaps Marianna had married thinking it would be a situation like her sister Madeleine, whose husband Rosario had gone to America while Madeleine remained in Sicily. Rosario would periodically return to Isola while sending a continuing stream of money from his fishing endeavors in America. But Marianna's parents told her that her husband Anthony would have no reason to return because all his people would be in America. Besides, they pointed out, he did not have Rosario's temperament to come back and forth. So when Marianna left with her husband, it was with the knowledge she might never again see her parents. She never did. Her mother lived to seventy-five years old and her father to ninety-five years old, he being killed in the bombing prior to the Allied invasion of Sicily in 1944. Her husband, Tony Russo, died in 1942 of a heart attack, so distressed was he that his beloved two countries were at war. During these trials, Marianna took her grief to God in her prayers, and as part of the Catholic tradition, would have daily offered her own sufferings to God, as a kind of prayer of trust and praise.

She did not return to Sicily until she was eighty years old herself, in 1964, when she could go by plane. Then she visited her four sisters and brother, learning from her sister Madeleine, her best friend as she grew up, that their parents cried and cried and rued for years that they had sent off their daughter, knowing they would probably never see her again. Marianna had not known that, and for many years she had felt abandoned. One wonders why they did not tell her about their own grief; perhaps they thought it would only make her feel worse, to know that they were missing her. Though in Pittsburg Marianna had found friends who were distant relatives, she was never truly comforted until she visited Sicily and heard from her sister that her parents were as unhappy as she had been at their separation. They never wanted her to go but thought that it was right for her to be with her husband. Learning that they did not easily abandon her helped heal her loneliness, even after sixty years.

Then Marianna's sisters and brother told her about life in Isola during two world wars, a major economic depression, Mafia repression, postwar traumas, and the fact that her, Marianna's, monetary assistance through those years was an important factor in seeing them through the many travails. In that little Sicilian town at the time of her visit in 1964, there was still no indoor running water. The electrical service was relatively poor, and there were no washers, dryers, and ranges such as were standard in the United States. Marianna saw that her life, tough as it was at the start, was substantially better than she could possibly have hoped for in Isola. When she came home from that trip, she kissed the floor of her kitchen, thanking God for having her parents send her off with her husband to the United States. She could never have imagined when she emigrated what a huge difference it would make in her life, in that of her family back in Sicily, and in the lives of her children born in America.

Present-day immigrants who miss their relatives as Marianna did, or anyone who misses family members due to separation, can follow her example of giving her grief to the God who loves us and go on with doing what needs to be done each day.

## *Alms for the Poor*

Many faiths suggest, or even require, that their adherents give alms above and beyond the donation to the parish church and care for the poor and underprivileged among them. The Catholic Church makes such a suggestion. Since the women in the family were the financial managers, they made the donation decisions. Grandmother Marianna gave specifically to causes for the poor, while my mother regularly gave donations to the orphanages in Sicily, year after year. Ileane and I have always given to our local church; additionally, I elect to donate to the seminary in India. We also sponsor a scholarship to one of the local Catholic high schools, so deserving students who are without means can attend. Our faith tradition teaches us that the gifts we have been given are to be used for the common good. It also teaches us not to give to God last, but first, and with a generous heart, trusting that God will bring all things together for our good. We do feel that we have received blessings and good fortune many times over.

# Prayers of Petition

Catholics and other Christians commonly ask others to pray for them and their concerns. My mother did the same; however, the others that she asked most often to pray for her concerns were not her friends and relatives, but our spiritual ancestors, the Saints, who are acknowledged as spiritual leaders and who, by virtue of miracles occurring through their interventions, are understood to be in the presence of God already. We understand that their closeness to and unity with God are the source of their power to lovingly intervene in human affairs.

My mother showed her commitment to her causes through nine-day prayers called Novenas, in which she asked for prayers from several patron saints or from Mary, the Mother of Jesus. Some present-day research has shown that prayer makes a difference in healing. Even if the persons of concern do not know they are being prayed for, those persons recovered more quickly and had fewer complications than the control group (Byrd 1988). My mother had no such research to support her faith; she just prayed Novenas constantly and saw their impact. The story that follows about my journey home after serving in the army is one incredible example of the power of prayer and of my mother's in particular.

# A Series of Interventions

In January of 1946, right after the first of the year, the army began sending people home from Japan. My mother had been constantly asking when I would be coming home, so in January, in one of my regular letters home, I wrote that, the best I could determine, it would be April or May of 1946. She did not like that one bit. On February 1, my mother announced to my father, grandmother, and other relatives and friends in the area that I would be home on February 15 because she was starting a fifteen-day Novena, and they never failed with anything that was justified.

She turned out to be right. On February 1, 1946, I was in Yokohama, Japan. On February 15 I was in Martinez, California. The situations that occurred to get me home on February 15 are incredible. Had any one of them not taken place, I would not have gotten home as she predicted. We consider that the events unfolded as they did due to my mother's prayers.

The following is a rundown of what it took to get me home on her announced date, of which I knew nothing. January 31 was a Saturday, so after a morning's work in the lab, one of the fellows, a Tech-5, suggested that he and I go for a sight-seeing trip around the Tokyo-Yokohama area. By this time I was a staff sergeant, so I had authority to use a jeep. After several hours of riding around, we found ourselves in front of the army post office. It was about 5 p.m. The other fellow suggested that we go in to see if they would give us Monday's mail. The noncommissioned officer there said we needed a staff sergeant to sign for the bag. "John's a staff," my partner on the trip said.

"Okay, sign here. Here's your mailbag. It's pretty full." We picked up the heavy bag and hauled it out to our jeep. We drove straight back to our headquarters and began sorting the mail. There were a lot of packages and large envelopes. The mess hall was open, and mess was being served. We went to eat and came back to finish sorting mail.

Near the end, the other fellow said, "Here's one for you. It looks official." I opened the envelope. It was an order to report to the replacement depot. After some discussion, we decided that the depot was the first step for returning to the States. It was now about 8 p.m., and in walked the commanding officer (CO). The CO had not come back to the orderly room on Saturday nights in weeks; this was the first time I could remember. The Tech-5 immediately approached the CO with the info that I had received orders to report to the replacement depot. The CO told the Tech-5 he might as well take me there, since I would not be doing anything before I left on Monday anyhow.

We arrived at the replacement depot at 11:45 p.m. The receiving personnel stamped the time and date on my papers and told me to report back at six in the morning, when we would board ship. All those at the depot before midnight boarded that ship, which was the fastest one in use from Japan to the West Coast; it took only two weeks. All arrivals after midnight left on the next ship, not departing till three weeks later. The later ship was not so fast and took more than three weeks to get to California. So in total time, I would have arrived a month later in California had I been twenty minutes later at the replacement depot.

The ship that I was on was headed for Seattle, where we would be processed for discharge at the convenience of the U.S. Army. The expected time of arrival was Sunday, February 15. However, a series of severe storms caused a change of port. San Francisco was to be our debarking port.

Then, another change: a one-week delay in berth availability had us further rescheduled for San Pedro, the Los Angeles port.

We arrived in San Pedro on Saturday afternoon, February 14, but as no space was available for the two thousand GIs to be processed, we were transferred from ship to buses to train. The train went up the valley all night, and we arrived about 8:00 a.m. Sunday morning at Camp Beale, which was about fifty miles from Martinez, across the bay from San Francisco. It was fifteen days from the beginning of the novena, the day my mother had announced I would be home.

Of course, I called home from the camp immediately. No answer at home. The Martinez telephone operator was the wife of a first cousin. I was not able to talk to her, but it turned out that her shift was ending a few minutes later. Since she knew the origin of the call, she made sure to inform my parents they had a call from Camp Beale. My mother told my father, "We have to go there."

My father was stunned. "Those army camps are big. How will we find him?" He was trying to reconcile the information with what he knew. "We got a letter a week ago which said he wasn't going to be here for another month or two."

He was in a state of shock at the news and did not argue much more. When my mother insisted, "He's there, let's go!" they went.

They arrived at the camp's main gate and asked for Staff Sergeant John Bellecci. At the time, fifteen thousand people were in Camp Beale. They did not have any record of the 929th Petroleum Laboratory, my outfit, or a record of my arrival, since we had come not from Japan but from Los Angeles. In any case they decided to humor my mother and called all the orderly rooms that had received people during the past twenty-four hours.

Meanwhile, I was walking around with three or four other GIs a short distance from one of the orderly rooms. All of a sudden I heard this plain, unadulterated scream. "Sergeant! Sergeant!" I looked around, and I found everyone looking at *me*. A major was determinedly striding toward me saying, "You're a poor example to your men: your tie is loose, your jacket unbuttoned, your hat in the wrong position. What's your name?"

"John Bellecci, Sir." It had become very quiet.

"What's your name again?"

I repeated it louder and emphasized "Sir." I apologized for my lack of proper dress with the excuse that for the past couple of years we had not been very formal. The major accepted my excuse and dismissed me with the advice that, now being in the States, we wanted to show the newer people what a first-class army looks like. "Yes, sir," I said.

Then one of the nearby GIs asked me who I was and said he thought that the orderly room had said my name over the loudspeaker. I had not heard it. I went to the orderly room and gave my name and was told that my parents were at the main gate.

"How can I get there?"

"The corporal will take you."

In the guard shack at the main gate were my parents.

My mother was telling everyone in the shack, "I told you he was here." My father had described the basis of their trip to Camp Beale. I recounted that I had indeed been in Japan two weeks before. They were all amazed. The OD (officer of the day) gave me a three-day pass on the spot and a phone number to call to see when my records would catch up with me at Camp Beale. It was nearly a week before the records arrived, and I was discharged on February 25.

After the drive home, this incredible series of events was retold often. My mother's praying and intuition were given high credit. The man across the street, Mr. Holmes, called me over, shook my hand, and thanked me for serving the country. Then he, a non-Catholic, said, "If your mother pulls another one of these, she's probably going to have some converts!" He was also amazed by the events.

## *It's Easier When You See their Strength*

In 1954, my brother Frank and his wife Joanne had a second child, Catherine, who was born with retinal blastoma, a malignant eye cancer. Very early in her life, Catherine had one eye removed and had only peripheral vision in the other. It was quite a shock and challenge to my brother and his wife, much younger than we were. Ileane and I, bearing our own loss of our third child, often wondered how they could stand to see their child in pain and having such troubles. They had faith in a God whose love does not falter. Frank was able to remain his usual buoyant self, trusting that if he did what he needed to do, it would work out.

Catherine turned out to have an independent spirit and a very quick mind. She did well in school and became fluent in French. With her family's support, she followed her love of French to attend the University of Paris (the Sorbonne), where she was successful in spite of such poor vision. When her vision deteriorated to blindness, she struggled emotionally to accept the loss. She finally set her mind to learning Braille and—after acquiring a seeing-eye dog—earning a master's degree in rehabilitation counseling.

Still later, she developed brain cancer in midlife, but Catherine's own faith in a loving God never wavered. Frank and Joanne took Catherine to Lourdes, with our daughter Lisa as her companion to get around. They prayed for a cure. They also prayed at the church in Paris where the incorrupt body of St. Catherine Labouré lies in a glass coffin at the side altar. Though neither the cancer nor her blindness was cured, Catherine's experience of God's love for her deepened, and she came home more at peace. Frank and Joanne and Lisa also felt comfort and peace at these holy places. Catherine has since passed on; our family remembers her lovingly as a strong and faith-filled woman.

## *When You Want Something More*

Though situations at work seem to pale when one experiences life-and-death issues as noted above, there came a time when I felt in a quandary about my job and its future. I turned to prayer for this as well.

Dow Chemical was a great company to work for. In 1960, I had four management peers with whom I could discuss plant problems; the company had a sense of optimism and progressiveness. My level of responsibility and the authority to go with it were well matched. I had the freedom to use my judgment without giving detailed explanations of every move, and I was able to institute several new ideas, two of which went into use at Dow plants throughout the world.

However, I did not see any place to advance within the Dow Chemical organization in Pittsburg. I had reached the top level I was going to reach there, for at least many years to come. Something within me wanted to do more. I had requested and been given some additional opportunities for trouble-shooting, one time making suggestions that improved a product beyond its design while keeping it safe and of high quality. I knew I could do still more.

I discussed this with my superiors, immediate and upper level; their responses left me unhopeful. They did not foresee any spot coming available in the near future, but suggested that if I wanted a higher position in the foreign division, I could move to Rotterdam or Australia.

How does one decide whether it is time to leave a comfortable job? I searched within, and knew I needed more of a challenge, and I wanted to make more of a difference with my skills. I did not know where this would lead but trusted that, if I did my best in whatever came up, it would work out all right. My wife and I both prayed for guidance, then we looked at the want ads. They listed only one true possibility, a job with Borden Chemical in Illinois as a plant manager. It was a relatively small plant, but it would call for a full spectrum of management skills. It would be the challenge I sought.

The support of my wife Ileane was absolutely essential, and it was positive. She told me, quite scripturally, "Wherever you go, I go." My parents, on the other hand, went berserk! My father had watched me leave the Corp of Engineers, Colgate Palmolive Peet Company, and Stauffer Chemical already. Since Dad had worked for one company for fifteen years, he always wondered if I had left those positions because I was about to be fired. However, he heard from my uncle, his brother-in-law, that I was greatly liked at Dow and did a highly regarded job there.

Still, he did not understand my need for challenge. What further challenge could be necessary, since I had already achieved the firsts of graduating from college and getting promoted within each company? My father wanted me to stay where the family was. He thought I should be satisfied wherever I happened to be.

This was a critical time for me, as I still felt a huge responsibility to abide by the Italian cultural tradition of being close to family and honoring the elders. Going against my parents' desires and expectations was hard to do, even though I was in my mid-thirties and had a wife and five children. Leaving a comfortable job seemed a foolish risk to many. I made the switch to Borden Chemical in Illinois based on the faith that God, who had created me with such skills and the desire to use them for good in the world, would continue to lead me in my life's work.

The plant in Illinois turned out to be a place in which I matured greatly in self-confidence and management abilities. After three years there, we returned to California, and I was capable of taking on more responsibility and authority at Occidental Petroleum in Stockton. Five years after that, Borden begged me to come back to work for them in Louisiana, where a much larger plant with significantly larger problems awaited. We *really* prayed about that move and again eventually decided to accept the challenge.

## *Guidance When Needed*

During the mid-1960s, when we were back in California and I managed Occidental Petroleum (Oxy), I named Cliff Mills as superintendent of one manufacturing department, and Dick Kirk of another department. But it was not working out. I could not understand what was wrong. Why were these really capable men not preempting the problems as I had expected they would? I wondered if I could possibly have made a mistake in promoting them. Something had to be done; it could not go on like this.

I went to Mass that Sunday and prayed for the wisdom to do the right thing: to know it, whatever it was, and to do it. As I walked out of church, it suddenly dawned on me that I had them in the opposite positions for which they were talented. One job was involved with calculations and precision, needing more of a mathematical mind who could analyze; the other job required big bulk production, needing one with machinery skills. I had assigned them to the wrong departments. I was more than a little apprehensive, though, knowing I would have to tell them they would be changing departments.

I told them I had prayed over this decision and informed them what it was. Much to my surprise, they almost got up and kissed me! They each knew they were not in the right place, but in no way would they have told their boss they did not want the promotion. They were not familiar enough with the big picture to know that they would each be perfect in a different department, but Cliff, a churchgoer himself, jokingly expressed their feelings, "John, the voice you heard was Dick and I right behind you, whispering in your ear." I was always grateful for this divine guidance and wisdom.

## Trust, No Matter What

My grandmother Ma did not see the positive impact her immigration to America made on her family until she went back to Sicily many years later, but she trusted God. I also was in a situation that was not really my choice, and I felt like I was being asked to trust God. I don't know if I have the depth of faith my grandmother did. I do know that I did not have to wait as long as she did to see the benefit of trusting God.

During my four years with Oxy in Stockton, California, it had been bought and reorganized twice. My third boss really wanted his friend Henry, then in Oxy's Florida operations, in my position. Unfortunately, even though I had the best production record and the best safety record in the whole Occidental company, this third boss was always nitpicking and finding fault. I could tell it would be just a matter of time before he really found something wrong, and he would have reason to let me go in order to get his friend in. I began to review other employment possibilities, both locally and within the state.

I was aware that Borden Chemical wanted me to work for them again, but it would be in Geismar, Louisiana, where they had a much larger portion of the production of Borden products, and also quite a few safety problems. I really did not want to move to Louisiana, yet other potential jobs had not been offered. Ileane and I really prayed about the best course of action. Rather than wait for the boss at Oxy to run me off, I quit. I accepted the Borden job in Louisiana during a visit over the Labor Day weekend. I started almost immediately, and my family followed me in October.

Henry actually did get my job at Oxy in September, but by the next spring was sent to Saudi Arabia to repair the ammonia manufacturing plant built by Chairman of the Board Armand Hammer as part of a deal. It turned out that I was at a chemical plant that had the same ammonia manufacturing problems as the Oxy plant in Saudi Arabia. But Borden gave me authority to do what was necessary to fix the problems, and in six months, I got the job done in Geismar. Everyone was amazed.

Meanwhile, my counterpart in Saudi Arabia had gotten nowhere in six months. The plant had faulty design and faulty equipment; it had never operated well. Henry was either unable to get equipment from the States, or, if it did arrive, he did not pay attention to the need to bribe the receiving dock foreman, so the equipment sat, unable to be accessed. Further bad news for Henry: Armand Hammer's purchase agreement with the Saudis to make the ammonia for them required their investment of twenty million dollars for the plant, but they still had nothing from it. Hammer's deal fell through, and he personally fired Henry. I had my plant running in good shape and my reputation greatly enhanced.

My lesson was obvious, and it showed up much more quickly than Ma's: Trust that what looks bad *now* really can work out for the best in the future.

## A Lucky Son-of-a-Gun

Often I would pray for guidance, and time and time again, the resolution of severe problems would suddenly fall into place. Ro Ventres, my superior for the two Borden tours, and Cliff Mills, my subordinate at three different companies, witnessed many of these situations and would say I was a lucky son-of-a-gun each time that would happen. How could I possibly have guessed, they wondered, that the situation would come about as I had predicted or expected? My secretary would say that I had played the odds. My answer was usually: "That's the only way it can correctly be solved."

Many such circumstances occurred. One of the first of important magnitude was at Colgate, and it involved getting the detergent plant online when we switched from our own manufactured active ingredient to one made by Chevron. It was supposed to make a better final product. We had to unload railcars and start the new process. My immediate superior forecast that we would have everything done and have full-scale product in a week.

I said, "No way. It's going to take us a week to get the cars unloaded, and we don't know what is in them." We had men working night and day because the cars had been loaded a month before and the active ingredients had settled down into a goo at the bottom, separate from the liquid. One consideration was to send it back and have them reblend it, but that would delay production by over a month.

One of our supervisors, Jack Coon, had an idea about how to stir it up, so we did get it unloaded, but it took a whole week. Then we had to make a sample of the new product and test it for several days before running at full speed. The people in the research department and sales department who knew how long it took other plants to do what we did thought it was phenomenal that we got it done that fast. My immediate supervisor, the production manager, was unhappy with me, but Mr. Stanberry, the plant manager, thought I had done a marvelous job by getting it done in two weeks. Jersey City and Kansas City had been working on the same problem for months. Later, I visited both plants to assist them in improving the quality and quantity of their production of this same product.

How were we able to come up with the right formula and plan when the others could not? I chalked it up to praying for wisdom every Sunday at Mass, wisdom to handle the job properly, and wisdom in listening to the people I dealt with.

## The Church Is More than Its Priests

My father did not often go to church when I was growing up. Sometimes my mother even missed Sunday Mass, but they always insisted we children go. We thought Dad did not go because of some problem with a church teaching, but later in his life, Dad did start going to church and to communion. (My mother wanted to tell him not to receive communion until he went to confession, but my brother Frank prevailed upon her to leave him alone and let him do what he was finally ready for.) We learned then that he found the priests at their parish to be rigid and uninspiring, but he still held to his faith.

A few years after his death, my mother wanted to donate a large sum of money to their parish for a specific purpose. The priest at the church in Martinez would not make time to meet with her. Startled, probably even insulted after all the years of her family's attendance and participation, she did not "wash her hands" of the Catholic faith. But she made a decision that seemed appropriate. She gave a much smaller sum in that church's collection and took her larger donation to another Catholic church in nearby Pleasant

Hill, which other members of the family attended. This was somewhat of a renegade action, since Catholics are supposed to attend the church in their geographical area. The priest at the neighboring town's church demonstrated more concern with the spiritual growth and daily needs of the people, however. My mother made that her Sunday Mass community and was eventually buried from that Catholic Church in Pleasant Hill.

I have known some people who quit the Catholic Church because their child did not get some special favor in the school, because they felt passed over for a particular volunteer job or ministry in the parish, or because they did not like the priest. We have a strong commitment to the Catholic Christian tradition and have been able to find a way to get our needs met and grow spiritually within the faith, using books, retreats, Bible studies, and various ministries in addition to the sacraments.

# A Living Faith

Many think of Italian Catholic families as being churchgoers and praying often. Our family fit this stereotype, and yet there was nothing blasé or routine in our faith. It was, and is, a deep faith in the abiding presence of a God of love, no matter what the situation seems like. What we received and experienced at Mass held, and continues to offer us, a constant hope in the Holy Spirit as a guide for wise and courageous acts. Our faith trusts in the saving power of Jesus Christ whose suffering, death, and resurrection provide a model for us to sacrifice and persevere, with prayer. Prayer is the foundation for our actions and is what we do in everyday life, not just in times of sickness. My wife prays for each member of our family on a daily basis.

I particularly found Sunday Mass to be my source of strength and conviction during the many times I was the lone voice advocating a particular course of action in my work. Though I was often considered arrogant or unfeeling for sticking to what I perceived as the right course of action, I would not reconsider just to be thought a "nice guy." I felt a responsibility to stay with the course of action at work that would prevent injuries and correct improper or faulty use of equipment.

Presently, I have the freedom in retirement to offer my service at Sunday Mass as a lector, and I enjoy this service very much. I have experienced the difference between "going to Mass" to fulfill an obligation versus being fulfilled, worshiping God, and feeling inspired at Mass. I am heartened when, during the preaching, someone relates the scriptures to daily life. I continue to seek ways to do God's work.

# *Bodily Healing that Amazes Doctors*

A torn Achilles tendon, a seriously infected foot, a heart attack, and the removal of an infected gallbladder while taking blood thinning medications— all these ailments befell me within a fifteen-month period. I was a person who hardly ever got colds, much less any illness. My wife put my name on the parish prayer line (that is a group of people who commit to praying daily for anyone brought to their attention), our daughter in Kansas put my name on the Dominican Sisters' prayer line, and my recovery was prayed for in churches in Louisiana, Kansas, North Carolina, Georgia, and California. The doctors were amazed several times in the various recoveries: (1) that I had the use of my new tendon (obtained from a cadaver); (2) that the infection disappeared from the end of a limb, usually very hard to treat; (3) that the heart attack did no lasting heart damage; and (4) that I did not die from complications following the gallbladder removal.

I did not know how close I came in the last incident. Apparently, the fluid buildup was so bad after the gallbladder surgery that the doctors advised my wife to call all the daughters to tell them it could be the end. A hospital social worker stayed with Ileane until at least one of our daughters arrived to be with her. All five came as quickly as they could, I was told. Our daughter who is a doctor left her clinic, the nurse her patients, and the one in Kansas got on a plane as soon as she could. The other two arrived at the hospital first.

My brother Frank and his wife Joanne were on a trip in the South and planned to visit us a few days later; Ileane called Frank with my status, and he and Joanne came immediately. One daughter was allowed to stay with me overnight in ICU; with a familiar person calming me, some sedatives could be discontinued. Against the odds, I recovered fully, and my heart remained in good condition even through the stress of complications after gallbladder removal.

After these illnesses I returned to lector at my parish and thanked the people at Mass for their prayers. At this point in my life, I believe I am still here because I still have something else to do. In all the situations I encounter, I pray, I try to do well, and I find that problems resolve in good time.

In this chapter, we have noted the faith of those who keep regular religious practices and of those who turn to God in prayer in time of distress. The effectiveness of both of these external and internal actions is seen in our continued optimism and persevering in daily life activities. To do this in spite of the many hardships enabled us to continue on the road to success. Those who seek faith, or who give God the time that can help their faith to grow, will find themselves better able to continue despite hardships.

# Chapter Eight: Manage with the Values

Immigrants who hold the values presented in this book and who act on them consistently will find themselves in leadership positions, either formally or informally, in the community or in business. But no matter what your sphere of life, whether raising children, supervising adults, or running a business, managing the people involved will call for problem-solving strategies and decisions that are unique to each situation, requiring your best attention. Those who use their skills and insight, and follow the values discussed thus far, can be closer to success. Anyone who says you must leave these values behind in order to achieve management success is mistaken. This chapter contains stories of just a few successful leadership decisions that illustrate the values specifically in business.

## The Toothpaste Detective

One never knows how a job assignment will turn out. It is important to have as your motto that honesty is the best policy, whether dealing with your superiors, peers, or subordinates. Though I was in a different business from my grandfather's fruit and vegetable sales in St. Louis, I, too, know from experience that acting with integrity will make all end well.

In 1949, early in my management career, I worked at Colgate Palmolive Peet Company in Berkeley, California. I was assigned the job of finding out why the company was losing several hundred dollars of dental creme per day. I was given four weeks and was expected to be sure and thorough. I checked all the scales with standard weights in the mixing department. I weighed all the empty bags, whose contents were dumped into the mixers to make the toothpaste. I counted every empty bag. I inspected the mixers before, during, and after every batch to be sure nothing was left in them. I vacuumed the floor and weighed the dust. I checked the standard weights. I never found an iota of an error. I weighed and measured all the raw materials. After almost three full weeks, I had discovered nothing. I consoled myself with the thought that I still had another week, but on Thursday I was told that Friday, the next day, I was going to another department.

Totally frustrated, I went to the filling lines with the idea of talking to one of the forewomen about possible thievery. While waiting for her to be available, I took a half dozen filled tubes off the line and weighed them. They were considerably overweight, but their weights as written were perfect. I weighed more; they were all over standard weight. Now I was really concerned because this meant that the women were the ones at fault, not doing their job. I had not had this impression of them and was disheartened to think I had to tell on them. First, though, I decided to talk to them.

When Lucy, the forewoman for whom I was waiting, became available, I told her what I had found. She said nothing to me but called the other two forewomen over. Then she suggested that we all four go see the department head. I did not know what to expect. We went in and closed the door, and Lucy said to me, "Go ahead, tell him the truth."

I explained to him that I had done all this checking and found nothing. But when I weighed the tubes of dental creme, I found all the missing toothpaste, and the records were not showing any overage at all. The department head asked the women if that was true. With some nasty words, the women stated they wanted the mechanics in the office. They were called in. Out came the vilest invective that I had ever heard women utter. They spent literally five minutes describing the abuse they had taken from the three mechanics whenever they requested that the machines be adjusted. The women were fed up with that abuse and called the men names I had only heard in the army. They were very angry and were not going to take any more abuse from the mechanics.

I was excused and later got a letter commending me on my work. The mechanics got letters of reprimand, and from then on, they adjusted the fill lines without a peep whenever requested. The three women later thanked me for having nerve enough to call the loss where it was. They needed someone to prove the only possible location of the loss of dental creme and then give them an opportunity to explain why. In this case, going along with Lucy's plan and honestly presenting all the facts gave them the opening they needed.

My next assignment, to improve production in a different part of the Colgate plant, called for a different strategy.

# *Starting from Scratch*

After figuring out why the Colgate company was losing dental creme, I was rewarded with an assignment to the sulfonation plant, a unit that worked with the raw materials for some of Colgate's other products. It was another problem area. I had heard that the previous supervisor had little interest in plant operations, but his level of neglect was clear when I found a mouse nest in his desk drawer. He had not opened the drawer in some time, obviously.

He also left no decipherable records. Operating procedures were scattered in different places, and the operators, the ones who actually attended to the functioning and output of the machines, spent most of their time doing nothing even if they had something to do. In order to get to excellence, I needed to start somewhere. I decided to start by listening to the operators.

I met with the operators one on one, and each gave me ideas on how to improve operations, offering considerably more help than I requested. Together, we compiled an operating manual, establishing procedures and duties to be used when the unit was operating and when it was not. This clarified job descriptions and expectations; now they could not say they did not know what they were to do. Next, I wanted them to increase their output. I didn't know them well enough to know if it mattered to them. I had to come up with a plan to help them know how well they were doing.

I began posting on the bulletin board the previous day's quality and quantity of product made, by shift. Word got to the union's chief steward that I was fostering competition among the shifts. It had not dawned on me it would be perceived that way. What I wanted was for the workers on each shift to know their performance of the past day, as soon as they came in, so that they would not make the same mistakes again. Ed B., the chief steward, came to tell me he was not going to have any competition among the shifts. He expected his size (six feet four inches), bulk (over 300 pounds), and position would be intimidating. I responded with a topic that mattered to him: I told him I did not want to issue citations for repeating poor performance. If the operators wanted to keep their job, they should know as early as possible what was not going correctly. This new perspective on the situation satisfied him. He agreed that if this posting reduced the number of citations, he would let it continue.

As it turned out, the operators already on the job had the abilities and willingness to work hard that I needed. We quickly improved our production. I rejected only one new operator after a reasonable training period, as he insisted that a thousand and ten pounds were to be written 1,000 10. Clearly, he did not know math and was only going to make mistakes in a place where math was a necessary skill. When the fellow insisted to Ed B. that he was correct, and I was trying to get him to make mistakes, Ed agreed to move the fellow out of the department without a union grievance.

In that situation, I was able to urge people toward excellence by listening to them and taking their ideas into account. I gained the respect of the union chief steward by showing my goals for excellence in production to be in tandem with his of continued work for the operators. In the next story, I force a crisis, and its outcome involves the same chief steward again.

## *No Poker Face with the Poker Players*

Some time later, while I still worked at Colgate, the graveyard shift foreman was sick. I came in to relieve the swing shift foreman at 1:00 a.m. Actually, I did not mind as it gave me a chance to continue my investigation on another production problem. I had already ruled out the lab and manufacturing as the source of the problem. Within a little time, I determined the error was in the packaging machines. Therefore I had the packaging lines shut down. The crew of ten who worked in this area spent almost two hours with me cleaning, scraping, adjusting, oiling, and checking the cartons until finally we were ready to start up again. However, it was a quarter to three and lunch was at three o'clock. I told everyone individually to go to lunch early since they had really applied themselves, but I expected them back at the end of regular lunch period.

At 3:20 a.m., the end of regular lunch period, half the crew did not show up. I was not completely surprised; I knew production was not what it should have been in that area, but had no proof before. I waited till 3:30, and then made sure I got documentation. I had the union's shift steward sign the slip of "no production" because I did not have enough people available to start up the machines; then I went looking. At 3:40 I found them playing cards. They scattered as soon as they saw me, and they all beat me back to the packaging line.

I told each of the five latecomers that I was turning in a citation for each. This is a formal complaint made to the union about their workers in our plant. It always involves some investigation and protest, so plant management will not issue a citation unless something is flagrant. I felt strongly that this was a flagrant abuse of the rules and that we needed to make the point in no uncertain terms. I wrote the citations up and had them in my desk drawer, ready to be submitted at 7:00 a.m. to the plant personnel manager, who informed the union chief steward of all citations.

About 6:00 a.m., one of the five men, the mechanic, Al, approached me about removing the supply man from the citation list. I said, "No way." The man in question was black, and the remaining four were white. I knew if I removed the supply man, the others would claim some sort of tokenism. But Al was sincere. He wanted the black fellow removed from the citation list because it was his third citation, which would result in his being fired. The other four on my citation list had no previous citations.

"Too bad," I said. But Al would not leave. The level of Al's concern caught my attention. I had the choice of holding a grudge or listening and negotiating. I did not know how long Al and the others had worked together or if he knew something about the supply man's financial situation, but he was not taking "No" for an answer. Since I was also aware of how the union usually reacted to citations, I decided I had incentive to negotiate.

I suggested that I would remove the supply man from the list, but the other four were not to contest the citations in any way. If even one of them did contest it, I would find the removed citation and include it also. I told him I had the shift steward's signature to verify which crew members were missing and that I had a shift foreman from the adjoining department also sign to confirm the men he had and had not seen. "I have you guys pretty well dead, so if you want to save his job, there will not be a meeting on this." I didn't know how the other three felt about the situation, but since Al was asking for another chance for the supply man, I figured he would take care of informing the other three.

Al agreed. "Okay, it's a deal."

When I turned in the four citations a few minutes later, the personnel manager went through the roof. Relations with the union had been going pretty well, but now four citations in one shot would definitely mean discord again. I told him not to worry; there would not be any meetings or repercussions. Then I went home to catch up on some sleep.

At about 2:00 p.m. I returned to the plant. Within minutes after I was in my office, Ed B. came in and wanted to know what threat I had used on the four men who had refused even to discuss their citations. That had never happened before, so I must have used some threat, he reasoned. Using all his height and weight, he promised that when he found out what it was, he "would be on my back, plenty."

I calmly and directly told him that they knew they were in the wrong and just did not want to make it worse. When he heard the word "worse," he cooled off considerably. Perhaps he thought that full exposure of the problem with the four might make it more serious for at least one of them. In any case, he left, and I never heard from him again about that particular incident. However, the assistant chief steward came by a few weeks later and said that he pretty much had the whole story and that Ed B. would not be bothering me or the department. Ed was too embarrassed to even come back and talk to me about it.

For my part, I learned the strength of concern the operators had for one another, which was a positive for our plant if it could be directed toward improved production. I also was extremely glad I had the insight to let go of any ill will toward the offenders and decided to negotiate. I did not think I lost any power by negotiating but felt instead that I had used my power wisely. This is important to remember when you come into power. There are always several ways to solve a situation.

## *Mercy Earns Cooperation*

Shortly after that incident, I was promoted to the position of Spray Products Department Supervisor. We had a serious error in charging (or loading) a crutcher, as the mixers are called in the soap industry. Ray B., the crutcherman (the one in charge of the functioning of the crutcher), with whom I got along well, called frantically for me on the loudspeakers which were heard on all five floors of each of three buildings. I went to the fourth floor where the control board and crutches scales were located. (These were platform scales that allowed us to weigh each sack before it was loaded in the crutcher.) Jack F., the fellow who cut and dumped sacks of dry ingredients, had erred by loading three times the amount of one ingredient and a third of the correct amount of another ingredient. Not only was this going to make a faulty product, but there was no way they could hide it from me, and once I saw it as it moved down the line, Ray and Jack would be up for reprimand. Jack was a hard worker, but illiterate, and if he lost this job, it would be hard to find another as good. Ray wisely called me immediately, before anything untoward happened.

I brought the crew together and told them we could save a lot of problems by revising the recipes, as formulae are called in the soap industry, but everybody had to do extra work. I said I would do the calculations for how much of the ingredients it would take to even out the mistake. Since we had two crutchers that dumped into a central tank, it was possible. But usually we had hours to mix up the recipe, and this time we did not; we had to get everything in the central tank in correct proportions before it moved the product down the line.

This is like correcting a mistake of putting too much salt (or other ingredient) in your home recipe. Since you cannot remove it, you must figure out how much of all the other ingredients you need to add so that the salt is at the right level. If you cannot, you must throw your food out.

We normally would have had to stop production to fix the mistake, but since Ray had reported it immediately, with my idea for revising the recipes, we could prevent that. The whole crew agreed to do the work, in hopes Jack and Ray would not be cited with a written reprimand. The lab was on notice that they would be running extra samples to give me feedback on how close the recipe was to the requirement.

For hour after hour we worked, through four rounds of loading the crutcher to balance the ingredients, mix them, then unload it and fine tune the recipe after getting feedback from the lab. The tower operator, the crutchermen, and a lab analyst worked with me steadily. We went through an ordeal to get back on line; the unit was upset, and the lab had many extra samples they had to run. Yet, with our combined efforts, the finished product was as good as we had ever made. My goal was met for a high quality product, but I was also deeply gratified with everyone's attention to precision in following orders and with the good communication between the departments up and down the production line. When the final product results were in, everyone could finally relax, and we went back to routine operations.

The department steward of course heard about the whole story. He came into my office to ask what I was going to do about Jack, since his gross error had caused considerable disruption and some lost production. I asked him: "Was anyone hurt?"

"No."

"Did the filling lines run out of product?"

"No."

"Did everyone really cooperate to prevent real disaster?"

"Yes."

"So what would I write in Jack F.'s citation? 'He made a mistake, but everything was all right.' Wouldn't that be pretty dumb of me?"

The steward asked incredulously, "You're not going to do anything to him?"

"No, I'm not, but I'll remember what you fellows can do when you want to do it," I warned with a smile. He left smiling as well. I remembered the favor my Latin teacher did for me when I needed an A to continue playing football. Her mercy did not cost her anything, and I worked harder than ever in her class, to make sure I would not go below expectations again. The result here was similar. I got a loyal crew out of it; they all worked better. Success occurs when you get the job done right and you can inspire people to do their best, even when errors occur.

# *One Million Dollars, in One Day*

In the previous situations at Colgate, when I first arrived at the new job, I took time to talk to the people involved before making any changes. That earned me their cooperation. But such an approach is not always possible. In the following story, I felt a little overwhelmed by the problems and thought I was being asked to do the impossible. My approach was out of the norm, and the value that motivated my decision was to be as assertive as necessary to do what was right.

When I arrived at the Borden plant located in Illiopolis, Illinois, in 1961, I noticed on my first tour some very dangerous situations involving highly flammable material. I could smell it because an operator was incorrectly transferring it from tank car to storage tank, but only because the pumps did not have enough pressure to transfer the product. Another safety mistake was the use of an open motor to transfer flammable materials. Those and other quickly identifiable problems made that plant a bomb waiting to explode.

As plant manager, I called Ro Ventres (the general manager, my immediate boss) and explained the extremely unsafe situation. He said to go ahead and fix it up. I told him I needed a million dollars—my off-the-cuff estimate—but my authority limit was one hundred dollars. Ironically, at Dow I could authorize a thousand dollars as a superintendent; here at Borden as a plant manager my limit was one hundred.

I communicated the urgency by telling him I had made the decision to shut the whole plant down temporarily. It needed to be fixed before we continued operations. If this was not agreeable, I was going to discontinue all operations permanently. He questioned that decision, "Well, you have these orders to fill!"

I retorted, "Not with this non-equipment!" He told me he would call me back, which he did a few hours later. He had good news.

"Fix it, and keep a good record of your expenditures. Make up the plant order requests, and bring them with you when you come to Leominster (headquarters) next week."

We spent $975,000 on proper-sized equipment, safety equipment, and spare parts that needed to be on hand. Usually it takes weeks of paperwork, not to mention approval by the board of directors, for that sum of money. So Ventres was sticking his neck out for me. However, he knew I was a good risk because I had worked with similar flammable petrochemicals and vaporizing gases at Dow. His willingness to risk, together with my knowledge and definite stance of not running an unsafe plant, made a good combination.

In this situation, my analysis of the situation was not one the board of directors wanted to hear, but it was what they needed to hear for a long-term satisfactory solution. Since I was on site and had expert knowledge, my superiors needed to trust my judgment, while I had the responsibility to make the long-term situation clear to them. The risk to me was that I was not being a "Yes" man. Those who want to be leaders will have to cultivate the courage to be assertive, and the wisdom to know when it is necessary.

## Don't Try to Take Advantage of Your Boss

Though upper management knows the big picture of what's going on in a company, the supervisor most closely connected with an operation usually knows its status best. In the following story, I was the person in management who knew best what our production quantity would be. I had a choice to make of using that information for either short-term personal advantage or a long-term reputation as a team player. Integrity said the choice would be the latter.

In September of 1974, working for Borden Chemical, but in Louisiana this time, I turned in to division headquarters our plant's production forecast figures a week ahead of the annual staff meeting, held in New York City. The Chemical Division Controller (the top person in charge of the accounting departments for all Borden's chemical plants) brought my paperwork with the forecast figures for the whole Geismar complex to the president of the company and chairman of the board, Gene Sullivan. This was an appropriate step. But because the figures for the ammonia plant were markedly higher than any that had previously been reported, when Sullivan saw the forecast at 270,000 tons, he did not believe it and would not accept it. He told the Chemical Division Controller so, in very definite terms. "If Bellecci lives up to that forecast, I'll kiss his *** in Macy's window at high noon."

The controller later told me how he had responded: "Mr. Sullivan, I think John would be embarrassed." (Macy's probably would not have been too happy, either.)

Sullivan's reaction was understandable, since part of his job as president and chairman of the board was to protect the price of the company stock. If he published an unattainable forecast, it would hurt the company on the New York Stock Exchange. He did not want to forecast profit if he was not certain the company could realize it, if not more. The ammonia plant was a major hub of the petrochemical operation, and its performance would affect the whole Chemical Division, and thus the Borden Corporation, pulling it either up or down.

The following week I arrived in New York along with the other group VPs. We were there to explain and justify our forecasts for the coming year. Mr. Sullivan took me on first, since he did not believe me, and he offered to bet me: for production over the forecast, I would win one dollar per ton from him, but if production went under the forecast, I would pay him a dollar per ton. I knew the improvements I had made in streamlining and efficiency in the ammonia plant, so I quickly calculated. I had forecast 270,000 tons but was certain we would make much more, up to 300,000 tons. That meant my boss would owe me $30,000. I felt confident in my response.

I said, "If we make what I really think, you will fire me, and if something goes badly, I couldn't possibly afford it." Since I knew he loved a good bet, I made a counteroffer. "However, I will bet you one dollar per *thousand* tons over or under."

"All right" he said, "I'll take that bet."

I kept to the values I held as important, and I won the bet. We absolutely demolished the forecast, going over it by 37,000 tons.

Max Minnig, the Chemical Division president, came to Louisiana in January and brought me Gene Sullivan's thirty-seven dollars. Thereafter, on an annual basis, Mr. Sullivan and I would bet ten dollars on the ammonia plant's production forecast. Since I was the one closest to the situation making the annual forecasts, I nearly always won. He always happily paid off. In fact, I think there were a few times when he paid twice for the same bet.

I never regretted not accepting his offer of a dollar per ton for several reasons. I think I would have been suspected of withholding information on purpose, perhaps in order to make some kind of personal financial advancement or to try to make myself invaluable to my superior. Also I did not want to have any one-time or continuing bets of that size with anyone. Even if I was sure of the outcome when our plant was running well, I could not predict any natural disaster or supply disaster. To have to pay that huge amount in case of either of those situations would have put my personal income and my family in jeopardy. It was not worth it to me. I wanted a clean reputation and a secure family. It is not success if you are putting your family's income at risk. Mr. Sullivan still enjoyed the camaraderie of betting with me, and I used my skills to advance the company.

## Give Strong Feedback about an Unworkable Plan

Frequently, people with the same level of responsibility are asked to share a job, a classroom, an office, or the administration of a program. This kind of team playing can work with people who have cooperative spirits, a similar or compatible knowledge base, and a clear delineation of responsibility.

Unfortunately, there might be times when it is necessary to oppose the team player plan. This story is about a time when I objected because of the lack of a similar knowledge base.

In 1987, the new president of Borden Chemical wanted to revise Borden by giving another group VP part of the Geismar operation, which up till then was under my sole administration. The notice of this change was sent when I was out of my office taking care of a problem the new president had generated. When I returned a day or so later, I was appalled to read of this plan, which I perceived as a total mistake. To split this site between two bosses when the proposed new VP did not know anything about managing in a non-Union atmosphere would invite chaos in management and procedures. Since Geismar was one of the big producers of the Chemical Division, the whole company would suffer. Having worked at Geismar since 1968, I felt a deep commitment to its success. I was determined that this change would happen "over my dead body." I became aggressive, not just assertive.

I called up the president, gave him a good piece of my mind, and told him I would be at his office in Columbus, Ohio, on the following Tuesday to straighten this whole thing out. This actually is quite risky behavior. A subordinate does not usually tell his or her boss how the organization should be structured unless asked for feedback. However, I was in my sixties, close to retirement, and if it did not work out my way, I decided I would leave the company. Additionally, I knew if this plan was brought to the attention of the board of directors of the Chemical Division, the president would be censured for causing a problem within a big money producer for the company.

The president, meanwhile, told the other group VPs that I was extremely angry over a change he was making, perhaps testing for their support. Ro Ventres, the VP who had worked with me the longest, advised him to listen to me. "When John gets angry, he is totally correct. Even the chairman of the board went along with his recommendations." When I felt strongly about a correct course, I was willing to let people know. In this kind of situation, I was somewhat like my grandfather John, inserting himself to ensure chaos did not happen in the fishing community.

On the following Tuesday, I went to Columbus, walking straight into the president's office. I had only pointed my finger and began to open my mouth when the president disavowed the changes he had proposed, saying it would only be if I wanted them. I then went two floors down to the corporate VP of Human Relations, who was "copied" on the original letter about the new VP. I was certain, due to the terminology in the letter, that he wrote had written it for the president's signature. However, he said he did not know anything about it. I left, still quite angry.

Yet the plan was scrubbed, and the Geismar plant management remained as it had been until I retired. An added irony: During the last two years of my employment with Borden Chemical, I was given the management of another division. Since my superiors were willing to add work to my job, it seems obvious there had not been a need at Geismar for two plant managers.

Notice the context of my very aggressive behavior: I knew that I could retire if necessary, so I had a great sense of freedom rather than fearing the outcome. I'm sure that freedom was part of my willingness to speak up passionately for what I believed to be the best course for the company.

## Improve Morale with Fair Organizational Structure

Changes in leadership help an organization keep up with innovations in production, transport, communication, new products, and the like. This is true in the business world, as well as for volunteers in organizations or associations. But any change, especially a major leadership change, causes unhappiness due to gaining or losing responsibilities. The person making the changes will thus be wise to match the responsibility, authority, title, and salary (or gratitude gifts, for volunteers) with the jobs the people are actually doing, to boost morale. This is tending to the organizational structure, which requires attention, close observation, and creativity in order to meet the needs of everyone involved. In the case below, it also required a level of strong assertiveness.

Since the Geismar plant was the hub of the Chemical Division of Borden, any decision I made usually influenced one or more of the other four Chemical Division departments. Upon retirement of the Fertilizer Division's president, I took over management of its manufacturing department. I knew organizational changes would be necessary, but did not know the extent.

It proved to be very difficult to get the management in the Fertilizer Division in Florida to break the old habits and procedures that were ruining their business. The people had been working together for twenty-five years and had become very loose with the structure. One person was permanently incapacitated but was drawing full pay and retained his title as if he were on the job. One young person was doing the work of his supervisor, at substantially lower pay, while that supervisor did not show up for work, taking virtual retirement while still on the organizational chart.

The top management admitted these and other existing procedures were counterproductive but delayed making the changes with dozens of excuses. They were unwilling to revise the job descriptions to align with present actual work done. The "buddy system" was too entrenched. I finally took a forceful stand; they gave my secretary the information needed to make a viable organization chart that could be used for proper title, responsibility, authority, and salary. Had I not intervened, nothing would have changed. With the fairer organization, attitudes improved as well. Within six months, the Borden Chemical Fertilizer Division became a viable force in the fertilizer industry and was considered lucrative enough to be purchased by another company at an amazingly high cost, which Borden could not resist. Administrative restructuring led to financial success for the company.

The initial negative reaction of those who had developed such close relationships over the course of many years was not abnormal. People often feel threatened by structural change. Explanations of how things will improve or become fairer or more efficient might not sway those who are comfortable with the way a situation is. But such a vision can be fuel for your assertiveness if you, as the manager, are in need of some reinforcement. In this case, once the changes were made, the people did experience them as fair, and production improved so dramatically that outside businesses noticed and wanted to buy that site.

## A Time for Every Purpose

In the previous stories, we've seen leadership use tactics of cooperation and restructuring to save a floundering situation. In this next story, we'll see that it is time for dismantling, for tearing down. Much past history and dedication, and many hopes and memories, are in every business and organization, so the dismantling process is usually avoided until it is long overdue. Being the one in charge of dismantling requires the values of assertiveness and integrity.

Overseeing Borden Chemical's poly vinyl chloride operations became part of my job soon after the restructuring noted above. I took my usual approach: I visited the sites, evaluated what was occurring, and learned what, if anything, needed to be fixed. After just one visit to each of the plants, I could see that immediate shutdown of the plant in Leominster, Massachusetts, was necessary, removing it from further operations. When I proposed this radical action, the Borden president said, "I guess we knew that was coming." That was even more disheartening. It turned out that my predecessor had retired early rather than shut down the plant where his friends all worked. The facility, at first outside of town, was in the middle of town due to population growth. This made it a safety hazard and caused pollution problems as well as traffic congestion with the heavy trucks and frequent railroad transportation. It should have been closed ten years earlier.

I have often wondered, when the board president "knew it was coming", why they brought me in to do the job. Perhaps they were still hoping there was a way to salvage it, that I might see some possibility that they had overlooked. But I saw none. I could only make a recommendation about transferring those on production in Leominster to other Borden sites that handled the same product. There were two—Geismar, where I worked, and Illiopolis, Illinois, where I had worked twenty-five years before.

I assessed that the Borden chemical plant in Illinois needed an immediate ten-million-dollar infusion to bring product quality and personnel safety close to proper standards. In those twenty-five years, they had made no improvements, only maintained at a minimum level. I learned that they were about to have one of their big sales contracts cancelled because their product quality had been so poor for so long. If that was cancelled, others would follow suit, and the operations at this site would be dead.

I received an emergency request to intervene. It turned out that the VP of the company about to cancel the contract recognized me from an interaction twenty-five years before, when I had saved his company by making a special order and shipping it out on the day they called. He was still grateful years later, and because of that long-past favor, he listened to my plan for the Illinois plant. He revised his decision to cancel on the basis of my immediate plans for improving the product.

In these situations, when people were dealing with their feelings of grief and loss, we still needed to do business. Reality was still reality, and I needed the integrity to follow through on a job no one wanted to do. Additionally, assertiveness was necessary, but not aggressiveness.

This chapter has shown that a person who manages or supervises others, whether paid or as a volunteer, does not need to discard the values previously discussed in the book but rather can use them in every decision. Integrity was called for in the toothpaste problem and in the temptation to bet big money with the boss. One can expect that excellence is a common goal of managers, but arriving at it might take different routes. Sometimes you will do best to listen and incorporate others' ideas as with the operator's manual, and at other times you will need to dictate what each person will do, as in the crutcher fiasco. In both situations, we achieved excellence.

Being willing to be assertive is a definite value for a manager, and the level of assertiveness depends on the situation. The stories in this chapter showed the need for levels ranging from a gentle but firm assertiveness to all-out verbal aggression. The latter, of course, is quite risky for someone in management. Use it sparingly and wisely.

Finally, managers need to be able to let go of grudges. Perhaps you have experienced a jolt similar to the one experienced in the card-player situation. I felt we had formed a bond in a hard job done well, but then felt taken advantage of as they extended their lunch. When I did not hold a grudge even then, but negotiated from a position of power, all of us benefited.

# *Closing*

People like to feel that their efforts have not been in vain, that their work has made some lasting difference and improved life for someone. The successes I have had with my family, in my career, and in my leisure activities have made improvements for many people. If this book helps you have a better chance at making gains similar to my family's gains, then I feel honored. I count it as double success, first in my life and then in encouraging you. The lessons I've tried to convey in these stories have helped my progeny succeed. If they help you, please pass them on to your family and all those you care about, young and old.

# References

Byrd, Randolph C. 1988. "Positive Therapeutic Effects of Intercessory Prayer in a Coronary Care Unit Population." *Southern Medical Journal,* 81(7): 826-829.